INSTITUTE OF HUMAN RELATIONS

YALE UNIVERSITY

BEHAVIOR THEORY AND SOCIAL SCIENCE

BEHAVIOR THEORY AND SOCIAL SCIENCE

BY FRANK A. LOGAN, DAVID L. OLMSTED,
BURTON S. ROSNER, RICHARD D. SCHWARTZ,
CARL M. STEVENS

PUBLISHED FOR THE INSTITUTE OF HUMAN RELATIONS
BY YALE UNIVERSITY PRESS, NEW HAVEN
LONDON: GEOFFREY CUMBERLEGE, OXFORD UNIVERSITY PRESS
1955

Printed in the United States of America by
Vail-Ballou Press, Inc., Binghamton, N.Y.

Library of Congress catalog card number: 55-8705

CONTENTS

FOREWORD

DURING the months when this book was written its authors were in the final year of a three-year term as postdoctoral fellows in behavior science at the Institute of Human Relations of Yale University. The main purpose of the fellowship program was to provide opportunity for training, teaching, and research in some of the better integrated parts of behavioral science and to explore the possibilities of wider integration. Recorded in this volume are some of the results of the explorations of this group.

It is a book about problems—containing no new data, it is published as a contribution to behavior theory. In a sense it is a tribute to the late Clark L. Hull, whose theory has been chosen as the starting point from which analyses of some of the problems have proceeded. In the last decade of his life Professor Hull had entertained the hope and belief that his theory could be extended to encompass a wide range of data from several social sciences. He realized that this would be a long and tedious task and that his theory might well undergo drastic revision before it could predict more complex forms of human behavior. Some of the points at which revisions now seem indicated are discussed here.

Other problems taken up in this volume stem not specifically from Hullian theory but from a wider stimulus-response point of view. All theories that view behavior from the standpoint of input-output or antecedent conditions–behavioral consequences are confronted with common problems such as choice of intervening variables and their operational definitions. Omitted from consideration are all nonstimulus-response types of behavior theory, including psychoanalysis, whose absence may be conspicuous to readers familiar with publications from the Institute of Human Relations. This omission, like some others, is due to lack of time for thorough study and critical analysis.

The postdoctoral fellowship appointments of the authors

were financed by a grant to Yale from the Ford Foundation in the autumn of 1950.

Mark A. May

New Haven, Connecticut
May 10, 1954

PREFACE

PREPARATION of this volume was a terminal-year project of the authors' three years of close association while Ford fellows in behavior science at the Institute of Human Relations of Yale University. We wish to thank the Ford Foundation, Yale University, and, in particular, Mark A. May, Director of the Institute, for making these opportunities available to us.

During our tenure as fellows, much was given and nothing demanded of us. Meeting throughout the first year, five days a week for several hours a day, we had a chance to teach one another portions of our various fields. We also had opportunity to attend, sometimes as a group, sometimes individually, courses or seminars in clinical psychiatry, mathematics, law, chemistry, symbolic logic, perception, learning theory, and sociology. During the last two years each of us has devoted part of his time to teaching in our respective departments.

In accordance with the interdisciplinary traditions of the Institute of Human Relations, senior colleagues gave generously of their time when asked to sit in on our sessions during the discussion of matters within their special competence. We gratefully acknowledge our intellectual debt to John Dollard, Clellan S. Ford, Clark L. Hull, Ralph Linton, Neal E. Miller, George Peter Murdock, Frederick C. Redlich, and Fred L. Strodtbeck, each of whom talked with the group on one or more occasions.

Of course, our indebtedness is by no means limited to those who had occasion to attend our sessions. We have profited from discussion with our colleagues Chris Argyris, E. Wight Bakke, Frank A. Beach, Wendell C. Bennett, Bernard Bloch, Claude Buxton, Leonard Doob, Isidore Dyen, John S. Ellsworth, Jr., A. B. Hollingshead, Carl I. Hovland, Friedrich Kessler, Floyd Lounsbury, Sidney W. Mintz, Rulon S. Wells, III, and Albert F. Wessen. Since it would be quite impracticable to attempt to indicate all those who have been of help to us in one way or another, the above enumeration must be viewed as but a partial one.

We are especially indebted to Mark A. May. He attended most of our sessions, and his wide knowledge of several fields in social science was always at our disposal. Determined not to dictate any course of action, he was ever ready to advise when asked. His knowledge of the pitfalls in interdisciplinary research guided us around a number of such difficulties, and his fruitful contributions to our discussions make him, in a real sense, one of the collaborators in this volume.

Our gratitude is also due Jane Brown, G. Sarah Greer, Ruth Hays, and Elizabeth Pulley. Mrs. Pulley typed an earlier draft of the volume, and Mrs. Brown has typed a number of succeeding drafts, including the final one. Miss Hays has read the entire manuscript and suggested many felicitous changes. Miss Greer, Executive Secretary of the Institute of Human Relations, has smoothed our path in numerous ways during our tenure of the fellowships.

Finally, we wish to state that not all parts of this book are completely endorsed by all five authors. We have had, and still have, diverse opinions on several major issues. Rather than insert minority dissents at such points, we have attempted to represent our different views within the text. Despite these divergences, we are gratified at the extent to which we have been able to attain consensus.

F.A.L., D.L.O., B.S.R., R.D.S., C.M.S.

New Haven, Connecticut
May 1954

CHAPTER 1

INTRODUCTION

WE share with many social scientists the belief that each discipline concerned with human behavior can profit by utilizing materials drawn from other social sciences. Many attempts at interdisciplinary cooperation have been made in investigations of specific problems. Another approach to integration of the social sciences entails exploration of methodological and theoretical barriers hampering the development of a comprehensive analysis of human behavior. This book summarizes such an exploration by representatives of anthropology, economics, linguistics, psychology, and sociology.

We have concentrated our attention on the prospects of using modern psychological principles of individual behavior in predicting human social phenomena. This required examining some general issues which confront any attempt to formulate propositions about human behavior in stimulus-response terms. Such propositions range from empirical generalizations to highly theoretical statements. We began with a stimulus-response framework because it provided a least common denominator. This framework admittedly is not the only one which can be used, and we are not entirely convinced that it is the most fruitful one available. Nevertheless it has proved a useful basis for our inquiry.

Along with our discussion of general stimulus-response theory, we have examined the particular S-R behavior system proposed by Clark L. Hull and his colleagues. Here we have considered some problems which would arise in using Hull's reinforcement theory as a major analytical tool for studying human social behavior. Our first step was to review the way in which this theory handles the experimental data on which it was originally based. We have not made an extensive critique of Hull's theory from the point of view of experimental psychology since our primary interest was to anticipate future difficulties in applying his theory to more complex events. We then explored possibilities of such generalization.

We had several different reasons for devoting so much attention to Hull's theory and its derivatives. Since this theory is an extensive attempt at a comprehensive account of behavior, it deserves study on its own merits. Moreover, an extension of Hull's theory to a wide range of data from several social sciences has suggested some important issues for the development of any stimulus-response analysis of human behavior. Finally, further study of those issues has in turn clarified some of the difficulties faced by Hull's theory.

The present work is deliberately limited in scope. First of all, we are by no means proposing a new comprehensive theory. It is simply beyond our ability at present to develop a theory which will make specific, testable predictions about a wide range of complex human behavioral phenomena. Indeed, we disagree among ourselves on the feasibility of constructing such a theory in the foreseeable future.

Another limitation of this work is that we do not examine all current theories or analyses of human behavior. For example, we do not extensively consider the works of Parsons, Shils, and their collaborators (1951), or Lewin (1936), or Skinner (1953), or many others who have studied general problems of human behavior. While we have often used the works of such men for a variety of reasons, we shall not scrutinize them in detail.

Finally, we do not claim that integration at a broad theoretical level is the only way to achieve interdisciplinary cooperation. There are other ways of doing this. One discipline may borrow one or several concepts or principles from another, or may work on a problem of interest to another. An example of the diffusion of one or more concepts is Murdock's (1949b) use of stimulus generalization in analyzing kinship systems.[1] Such concept borrowing, when the investigator has

1. This use was not an application of Hullian theory to generate predictive theorems about cultural phenomena, but an instance of appropriation and adaptation of an empirical generalization developed by another science.

adequate knowledge of both borrowing and lending theories, can have a salutary result. Nothing, however, could be more destructive of the aims of integration than the taking over of mere phrases by superficial analogy without due regard for their original definitions or proper theoretical consequences (Olmsted, 1953; Moore and Olmsted, 1952; Olmsted and Moore, 1952).

With this orientation, our book proceeds along the following lines: In the remainder of this chapter we briefly state our view of theory construction and its relation to integration in the social sciences. In Chapter 2 we outline the major characteristics of Hull's theory. Rather than give an extensive exposition of this theory, we state only those concepts and propositions which are necessary for the remainder of the present work. Since any stimulus-response analysis requires a reliable way of defining, classifying, and measuring responses, we examine in Chapter 3 the several different methods of doing this which have been used in the social sciences. In the fourth chapter we consider several stimulus conditions which experimental psychology has found to be important determinants of individual behavior. Then, in the last four chapters, we discuss some specific problems involved in making a stimulus-response analysis of human behavior and, wherever possible, indicate some research which we believe would be valuable in solving such problems. Chapter 5 is devoted to language; Chapter 6 concerns what we shall call free behavior situations; and Chapter 7 discusses social interaction. Finally, in Chapter 8, we consider some areas in social science to which stimulus-response theories are most likely to prove applicable.

Some Aspects of Theory Construction

Since this essay is concerned with theoretical integration, it will perhaps be helpful, if only for pedagogical purposes, for us to state at the outset our understanding of the terms "theory" and "integration" and their interrelations.

Since we accept successful prediction (Spence, 1944, pp. 47–8) as a goal of behavior science, questions about theory may be approached in terms of the relevance of theory to such prediction. Prediction, which consists in statements concerning some future state of affairs, by its very nature involves assumptions as to at least the partial nonuniqueness of phenomena. He who would predict must therefore make some judgment, somewhere along the way, that some phenomena are the same or partially the same and that others are not; i.e. he must classify. Most adult human beings possess a ready-made mechanism for making such judgments, namely a natural language. By talking about things we classify them, whether we recognize the fact or not. This is a fact of some importance, since we are entitled to ask if any given set of statements, whether it be of a ready-made "folksy" variety or any other, is an efficient implement in the work of predicting.

The term "theory" has been defined and interpreted in many different ways. Everyone agrees that a theory is, among other things, a set of statements; there is disagreement about what other characteristics any set of statements must have in order to be labeled "theory." In what follows, we outline our view of these additional characteristics.

The ultimate test of any theory is the extent to which the predictions resulting from it are confirmed. To minimize disagreement as to what predictions legitimately result from a given theory, certain ground rules have been adopted. These ground rules include the principles of logic and mathematics, and help reduce ambiguities by the partial restriction of natural language. Their introduction follows from the application of a still more basic convention, namely that scientific activity should be replicable by other investigators. An ambiguous term can be as injurious to replicability as an undescribed piece of apparatus. Another value of the ground rules is the additional analytical power they often provide; e.g. in economics the rules of mathematics permit deduction from maximization postulates of many meaningful restrictions on price-quantity data.

Those statements of a theory used as premises in the deductive process are its postulates. Some of these may be directly testable; some may not. The postulates may be based on data, and these data may come from the theorist's own field or from other fields. The rules of deduction drawn from mathematics and logic also have the status of postulates, although they are not generally stated *in extenso* in theories. Those things taken as given, plus the rules of deduction, are then its postulates. The logical consequences of the postulates are theorems. Ideally, the postulates should be "(1) as *few* as possible, (2) *consistent* with each other, and (3) *sufficient* to mediate the deduction [of] theorems" that correspond, operationally, to all relevant data (Hull et al., 1940). Theories that attempt to predict natural phenomena generally fall short of this ideal.

In viewing a theory as a set of statements we made no commitment as to whether the statements are made up of morphemes from a natural language or of items from the restricted languages of symbolic logic and mathematics (Samuelson, 1947, pp. 23ff.; Arrow, 1951, pp. 129–54). As a matter of fact, as we have seen, the natural language of some investigators is used unintentionally for this purpose. However, serious disadvantages can be shown to inhere in such a procedure, which is undertaken in the belief that the investigator's audience speaks his language and ought to have no difficulty in interpreting his statements. Partially from the abundant evidence that this is not always the case has come the development of symbolic logic and its increasing use as a tool in theory construction. Natural languages possess many ambiguities which are largely but not entirely resolved by the considerable redundances furnished by the context. Also disadvantageous is the process by which the research worker classifies phenomena together only because they happen to be classified together as a result of their common nomenclature in his natural language. Instances in which this procedure is fruitful become increasingly rare as a science develops.

From such difficulties has sprung the conviction that the unambiguous definition of concepts (propositional variables) is a desideratum. Two kinds of definitions may be distinguished: the formal and the operational. Formal definitions of the sort termed "explicative nominal definitions" by the logician consist in placing the term to be defined on one side of an identity sign and some other term or terms on the other. These other terms may be previously defined or may be undefined notions (primitive terms), chosen either for their transparency or for their extreme difficulty of definition. Formally speaking every system has at least some undefined terms, unless it is characterized by circularity of definition, which is prohibited by the ground rules. Formal definitions, then, are purely theoretical, i.e. verbal or pencil-pushing activities, and are most useful in and around those postulates that state the logical and mathematical assumptions of the system.

There remains, however, the problem of connecting with the data the set of statements that constitutes the theory. This connection and its absolute necessity are hallmarks of science as opposed to formal systems, which are said to have no empirical content. Such connections are conventionally established by what have been called "operational definitions." Since the time of their description by Bridgman, twenty-five years ago, these definitions have been sharply attacked by philosophers, who have not, however, provided us with any other way of making the necessary link between the statement and the datum. Stevens (1939) in a classic paper pointed out the indispensability of operationism to behavior science. In brief, the method involves the specification of certain behaviors (operations), such as reading a pressure gauge, some results of which are defined to constitute an instance in the data corresponding to a particular concept in the theory (Bergmann and Spence, 1941).

With a set of postulates characterized by careful formal and operational definitions and a judicious choice of undefined terms, the investigator may, ideally, derive theorems or logically proved propositions from his postulates according to the ground rules provided by the formal postulates. The goal is to arrive at theorems which concern interesting phenomena and are testable. In this way the several postulates are brought to bear in a particular set of circumstances, and the theory delivers a prediction to the investigator.

Since the concepts are operationally defined, the theory specifies what results should be regarded as supporting the theorem and what should be taken as failure of prediction. It is characteristic of loosely formulated theories that in some circumstances any result is taken as support of one theorem or another. These theories thus "explain" after the fact whatever happened, but can deliver no predictions. No theory known to us can predict in all situations, or with 100 per cent probability of success in any situation; the difference between theories is thus one of degree. It can merely be asked of the theorist that he try to confirm only testable theorems and that he be prepared to accept the consequences of failure of prediction.

Failure of prediction ought ideally to indicate the falsity of one or more postulates. Actually, in the behavior sciences failures are often considered traceable to inadequate observational techniques, "folksy" or nonoperational definition of concepts, incorrect derivation of theorems from postulates, insufficiency of the postulate system, or inconsistency of the postulates. There can be many a slip between postulation and observation, and it is often difficult to ascertain precisely where the trouble is to be found.

Much of the development of science has consisted in empirical work supported by a minimum of theory. Requiring only the definition of concepts, this activity can then proceed to classification by one criterion or another and the correlation of certain data with other data. It is a type of research which plays a great role in the beginning stages of any science, since the generalizations (empirical laws) arrived at form the basis for many of the crucial choices of postulates in the succeeding construction of theory; it is less profitable, however, in later stages, when unifying theories have been constructed which offer predictions about wide ranges of new phenomena.

In most situations involving human behavior we are at the empirical law-gathering stage. The empirical generalizations sought have tended to be of two varieties: on one hand, the correlation between earlier stimulus conditions and later behavioral results, and, on the other hand, the correlation of behavior at one time with behavior at a later time (Spence, 1944).

It should be obvious that theorizing activity does not proceed in a vacuum. Definition of concepts is highly dependent on available observational techniques; postulates concerned with such concepts must be framed with an eye to the logical derivation of testable theorems; and the character of the postulates serves as a guide to the development of new observational techniques or the refinement of those already existing. Such interplay is constantly under way in any vigorous science.

Formal Integration

This book represents a circumscribed attempt in the direction of what we here call formal integration. Confusion and disagreement over the meaning and significance of interdisciplinary integration are apt to arise in part from the circumstance that there are at least three categories of integrative activity: formal integration, pedagogical integration,[2] and policy integration.[3] As will be evident, this tripar-

2. "Pedagogical" integration, as we use the term, is concerned with curriculum arrangements, more particularly with the attempt to design interdisciplinary (as opposed to the traditional departmentalized) science courses. In good part, "integration" in this context consists in rationalizing the whole course design in terms of some agreed-upon set of pedagogical objectives, both of the course itself and of the larger program of which it is a part. In any curriculum context it is, to be sure, a useful exercise to make objectives explicit and to attempt a systematic appraisal and rationalization of the course design in terms of these. However, in the attempt to design an interdisciplinary science course this process is a virtual necessity and must be reckoned as a major part of the integration to be done. For in such a case policy decisions must be made with respect to the relative time weighting and sequence of the various course components gathered often from widely disparate disciplines. This demands the development of an explicit framework in terms of which the disparate disciplines can be related one to the other for pedagogical purposes. Lacking this, the attempt to design interdisciplinary science courses is often predicated upon such pedagogical objectives as better student motivation and better continuity (whatever that may mean), which are supposed to be peculiarly attainable via a particular curriculum arrangement.

This brief aside on the matter of pedagogical integration has the simple objective of warning that disagreement and confusion over the meaning,

tite categorization is not a tight one. For example, the results of formal integration, once accomplished, will manifest themselves in the classroom and in policy decisions. Nonetheless, a recognition of these distinctions is helpful. The meaning of formal integration of theories can best be understood by first discussing the relations between theories.

The statements comprising any theory may be divided into two general categories: 1. those statements of attributes of and relations among phenomena which the theory takes as given (one of the two classes of elements previously referred to as postulates), and 2. those statements of relations among and attributes of phenomena which the theory attempts to explain.[4]

In these terms any two theories, A and B, may be related in a number of ways:

1. The theories A and B undertake to explain at least some of the same phenomena.

2. The theories describe and explore the consequences of at least some of the same given elements.

3. Theory A attempts to explain some of what B takes as given, and B describes and explores the further consequences of some of what A explains.

4. A final relation may be distinguished as conceptually somewhat different from the preceding in that it refers less

---

significance, etc. of integration of the sciences may arise if one party to a discussion has in mind the problems and objectives peculiar to the pedagogical side of the matter whereas another party is considering some quite different set of objectives and problems.

3. Numerous policy decisions (e.g. economic and political) require knowledge of the limitations and probable consequences of these decisions, which is often best gained from specialists in various sciences. Here integration requires that specialists express themselves with respect to the consequences of alternative policies and that their estimates be presented to the policy maker. Policy integration, so conceived, is to be distinguished from the process of normative evaluation which often must accompany a policy decision. Normative evaluation is concerned with resolution of conflicts between the ultimate goals or objectives of the policy decision, as opposed to simply predicting the probable outcome of the policy decision.

4. An event is said to have been explained if a proposition predicting its occurrence has been deduced as a theorem from a set of postulates and the event is indeed observed as predicted. Henceforth, circumlocutions intended to distinguish between the formal theory and its phenomenal referents will be dropped.

directly to the phenomenal reference of the theory. Some of the research techniques peculiar to one discipline (e.g. interrogation techniques) and/or some of the formal properties of its theoretical formulations (e.g. particular mathematical techniques or formulations, previously referred to as a part of the postulational structure) may be fruitfully applied to the study of phenomena with which another discipline is concerned. (We refer to research techniques and formal properties of systems which may be more or less peculiar to the disciplines in question rather than to such of these as are the common property of all scientific disciplines.)

Relations among theories are states of affairs existing at some point in time. Formal integration of two related theories consists of two things: 1. simple awareness of the relations listed above, and 2. extension of relations, including modification of the theories when they contradict one another. For example, A implies a proposition contradictory to one postulated or implied by B. In any such instance both A and B cannot be correct about the point in question, and the discovery of the contradiction presumably compels an attempt to discover the source of error.

A number of reasons or motives for formal integration can be distinguished. Some of these comprise a straightforward pragmatic aim to increase the confidence of the various theorists regarding the truth value of their respective postulate-theorem structures. Suppose theory A implies as a theorem a proposition which is a postulate in B, and from which B has yielded verified theorems. The benefit of integration (in the sense of discovery of this relation) lies in the increased confidence of both theorists in the truth value of their respective postulate-theorem structures. Another clear aim of formal integration is to search for more adequate conceptual orientations, theoretical approaches, and research techniques. This search often begins when the scientist discovers that he cannot satisfactorily answer particular questions or when he suspects that the kinds of theoretical tools and data with which he is familiar may never be adequate to the task. Thus may begin the search for new conceptual categories in terms of which to attack old problems. Finally, one other motivation for integrative activity may be mentioned, namely the aesthetic. Suppose that from the postulates of theory A we can deduce, as theorems, the postulates of theory B. If for the moment we define a new theory, AB, it will now have fewer postulated (unexplained) relations than did the old theories A and B taken together. In other words, the combined theory is more parsimonious than were the two previous ones taken together. It is true that if such an integration is achieved new and independent evidence will have been brought to bear on the truth value of the propositions comprising both A and B. Aside from this, however, the benefits of the procedure may be largely aesthetic; that is, the new theory AB may contain no more and no different propositions than did the old theories A and B taken together. And there may be no diminution in the knowledge, skills, and work necessary to arrive at those propositions in the new theory AB which before were separately the concern of A and B.

This enumeration of the motivations for formal integration could be considerably extended. However, it is perhaps wise to cut it short at this point, since for most scientists a discussion of the possible merits of integrative activity proceeds best in terms of particular examples, some of which will be found in the balance of this book.

CHAPTER 2

HULLIAN THEORY

IN considering problems which arise in extending stimulus-response analysis to human social behavior, we have started with the methodology and theoretical formulations of Hull (1943a, 1951, 1952), Spence (1951), Miller and Dollard (1941), and Dollard and Miller (1950). However, we wish to assert that this theory is not at present adequate for the successful prediction of social behavior, an assertion which will be documented throughout this book.[1]

Nonetheless we have used the Hullian approach in analyzing the problems facing behavior theorists, since it is a major attempt to treat behavior in exact terms. We shall therefore describe this method of theory construction and the fundamental features of Hull's model. This description will lead to two related topics important for understanding this approach: 1. the relation of Hull's theory to physiology, and 2. the problem of quantification.

Intervening Variables

The intervening-variable approach to theory construction begins with the proposition that behavior science seeks to predict how an organism will behave in a given environment, or, in different terms, which responses will be evoked by certain stimuli. Such predictions are to be made from two types of statements. One concerns what the organism has done in the past when confronted with various stimuli and what the consequences of his responses[2] have been. The second type

1. The reader should not infer that our failure to analyze critically any particular feature of the system necessarily implies our endorsement of that feature. Many discussions which preceded the preparation of this manuscript are not explicitly reflected in it, and some matters have not been dealt with because they appeared systematically either to follow or to be tangential to the central problems with which we are herein concerned.

2. By consequence of a response we mean an event which temporally fol-

of statement treats behavior in a given situation as a function of the organism's prior experiences, taking into account the degree of similarity between present and past situations. Both types of statements concern empirical phenomena: the first gives the organism's past history, and the second summarizes, in the form of empirical laws, relations between observed data. By combining the empirical laws with the specific statements about the organism, predictions can be deduced as to the latter's future behavior. The question now arises, how should the general statements regarding behavior be organized? Should they be left as empirical laws, or should they be cast into some other framework advantageous for making predictions?

The intervening-variable position proposes that the general laws be organized in terms of a model, or constructed organism, which will have all the input-output properties demanded by these laws. This is accomplished by relating certain classes of stimulus or antecedent conditions [3] to one or another variable in the model. These variables in the model are termed "intervening variables" and must be related in turn to others which are themselves related to measurable aspects of behavior. The transition between intervening variables defined by antecedent conditions and those defined by response measures can be made by means of still other intervening variables, which bear unambiguously stated relations to the two former sets.

The development of an intervening-variable system should follow certain restrictive rules. First of all, each intervening variable should be defined operationally. It should be unambiguously related to empirical operations or to other intervening variables which have been defined in terms of experimental operations. This does not mean, however, that the first definition is the final one. Intervening variables may be partially defined and further content may be added to their

lows a response without regard to any possible causal relation between event and response.

3. By stimulus conditions is meant the immediate environment in which the organism is operating; antecedent conditions refer to the organism's past experience.

definitions as research progresses. Secondly, as new laws of behavior are discovered, a model composed of intervening variables may change in its components or in their relations in order to conform to observed stimulus-response laws. Some of these new laws may be deduced from the model; others may not be deducible and may therefore demand modification of the model. A final restrictive rule is that the model should contain as few intervening variables as possible. Every independent empirical operation could be represented by an independent intervening variable; but this situation would make an intervening-variable model a mere exercise in choosing synonyms for each of a number of terms.

This method of theory construction, then, proposes that a set of hypothetical interrelated intervening variables be defined, directly or indirectly, in terms of stimulus or antecedent conditions on the one hand and response measures on the other.[4] An adequate system will successfully imply the input-output relations discovered as empirical generalizations on the behavior of actual organisms.

By design, this initial discussion of intervening variables has been rather general. A more detailed discussion of their development and use will be best understood after the reader has had some introduction to the Hullian system, a brief summary of which will now be presented.

The Hullian Theory

The Hullian theory [5] considers behavior as the event to be described and predicted. Behavior is viewed as a response

4. See above, p. 6. The reader should recognize, however, that an intervening-variable system may properly contain some constructs which specify state characteristics of the model organism, and that these characteristics need not be explicitly related to stimulus or antecedent conditions. In the Hullian system, for example, the concept reaction threshold (sLr) represents such a state characteristic. Similarly, the parameters of the several equations in the system partially reflect individual differences which are not dependent upon any specifiable stimulus conditions. A part of the quantification problem is to identify means of estimating the values for these state characteristics. Until such time they are useful only if 1. their relationships to the response terms are explicitly stated, and 2. they do not *differ* in value among the groups of organisms being studied.

5. We will not present the system in postulate form nor will we give a

(R) of the organism evoked by the stimulus complex (S) impinging upon his sensory apparatus. The theory, then, seeks to predict R when S is given. This prediction is accomplished by using intervening variables which are related to observable stimulus and antecedent conditions on the one hand and to observable response measures on the other. Values of the S conditions are transformed by the system into values of intervening variables, and these in turn are transformed into values of the R dimensions.

An S initiates a stimulus trace (s) which is related to the qualitative and quantitative aspects of the stimulus complex. Hull assumed that the trace increases rapidly and then decreases more slowly with the passage of time after the onset of S. The R bears a one-to-one relationship to a hypothetical intervening response (r). According to this scheme,

$$S \longrightarrow s \text{ - - - } r \longrightarrow R,$$

the prediction of R from S becomes a problem of predicting r from s. This is performed by the rest of the theory.

The r is a function of response tendency ($_s\hat{E}_r$);[6] r, and hence R, is assumed to improve monotonically with increases in response tendency. Improvement in R is reflected by an increase in its probability, amplitude, etc. That is,

$$S \longrightarrow s — {_s\hat{E}_r} — r \longrightarrow R.$$

Response tendency is defined as a function of the interaction of several intervening variables which are related to observable stimulus and antecedent conditions. Some of these

---

complete exposition of its applicability to the several areas of psychological inquiry. Such a presentation is beyond the scope of this document and is available in the references cited above. We will offer, instead, a minimal outline of the theory as it has previously been published, without reflecting those further modifications which any of the present writers favor; e.g. while our discussion of "reinforcement" will offer a possible alternative definition of this concept, we shall state in this chapter only those definitions already published. Accordingly this summary should not be taken to represent the theory which the writers would ultimately apply to social behavior.

6. Hull wrote the subscripts in capital letters. Because the small-letter subscripts are more appropriate to his system, and also because of printing simplicity, they are used here throughout.

variables act to increase, some to decrease, response tendency; the three positive ones are habit, drive, and incentive.

The associative (learning) intervening variable is called habit (sHr) and is assumed to increase toward an asymptote according to a negatively accelerated monotonic function with the number of reinforced trials (N). Thus the two necessary and jointly sufficient conditions for the accretion of habit are: 1. a reinforcing state of affairs following 2. a trial. A trial is the temporal contiguity of the s and the r. The concept of reinforcement may be viewed as a category of states of affairs into which an event is placed after research has shown that its occurrence on one trial is followed by an increase in the probability of a repetition of that R on a subsequent presentation of that S.[7] Hull, and Miller and Dollard have adopted the specific hypothesis that reinforcement is a drive reduction; i.e. that an event is reinforcing if and only if some drive (defined below) is reduced.

The second positive component of response tendency is drive (D). The primary drives are related to deprivation of food, water, or sex, or to the physical intensity of an applied noxious stimulus.[8] All drives present at any one time in the organism summate to form the total drive which contributes to the tendency to perform any and all responses attached (via habits) to the S. However, each drive is assumed to provide, according to its level, a characteristic drive stimulus (S_D); behavior specific to particular drives is mediated by this mechanism.

The final positive component of response tendency is incentive (K), which is dependent partially upon the magnitude and the time of delay of the reinforcement following a response, and partially upon the number of times the organ-

7. The reader will recognize the circularity involved in this definition *on the defining instance.* One cannot identify a reinforcement only by its effect on behavior and then hold it to be a determinant of that behavior, since prediction would clearly be impossible. The theory escapes this circularity by identifying a reinforcing state of affairs on one occasion and then generalizing in a noncircular fashion that this state of affairs will act as a reinforcement on all other occasions (see Chap. 4).

8. Miller and Dollard (1941) define drive as a monotonic increasing function of the intensity of any stimulus. They also favor the position that each drive is specific to the habits acquired on the basis of it.

ism has experienced these reinforcement conditions. Incentive, drive, and habit are assumed to interact multiplicatively in determining excitatory potential (sEr), which vanishes if any component goes to zero. Since sHr approaches an asymptote as a function of the number of reinforcements, sEr must also approach some asymptote.

A previously neutral stimulus which repeatedly precedes a noxious one acquires motivating effects; this secondary motivation contributes to the total drive. Similarly, a previously neutral stimulus will acquire secondary reinforcing effects if it repeatedly precedes a primary reinforcing state of affairs. Both secondary reinforcement and secondary motivation are presumably acquired according to the postulates of the system and are subject to ultimate extinction if the conditioning sequence does not occasionally occur.

Thus excitatory potential has three major positive components, habit, drive, and incentive, each of which may be affected by the learning experiences of the organism. Two variables oppose excitatory potential: conditioned inhibition and work inhibition.

Conditioned inhibition (sIr) accrues as an increasing function of the number of nonreinforced trials. Extinction is thus deduced on the basis of an increase in conditioned inhibition rather than a decrease in habit. Work inhibition (Ir) accumulates with the performance of any response according to the work involved, and dissipates as a function of the time of rest. Work inhibition is developed on both reinforced and nonreinforced trials; it accordingly temporarily facilitates the extinction process. Conditioned inhibition and work inhibition each subtract algebraically from excitatory potential. The remainder, called effective excitatory potential (sĒr), is considered the maximum value of response tendency possible at given levels of training, motivation, and reinforcement.

Effective excitatory potential, however, fluctuates [9]

9. While this fluctuation, at the present stage of development of the theory, is partially a residual factor resulting from errors of measurement and the effects of currently unknown determining variables, it is also held to be partially a basic characteristic of the model organism. That is, while the variance

through time; response tendency is the effective excitatory potential present at the time of observation. This is the result of positing oscillation (sOr) as a normally distributed, randomly determined variable which changes from moment to moment according to this distribution, and of defining response tendency (sÊr) as the algebraic subtraction of oscillation from effective excitatory tendency.

All associative variables (habit, secondary motivation, incentive, and conditioned inhibition) relevant to any stimulus generalize to any similar S according to a negatively accelerated decreasing function of the difference between the latter S and the original S. A subject thus can learn to discriminate between similar stimuli only on the basis of differential reinforcement which increases habit to the positive (reinforced) stimulus and increases conditioned inhibition to the negative (nonreinforced) stimulus in order to offset the generalized habit. The conditioned inhibition, of course, generalizes in turn upon the positive stimulus, and accordingly the ease of forming a discrimination is an increasing function of the difference between the positive and negative stimuli.

Whenever several competing R's are attached to an S, that R is performed which has the highest momentary response tendency. Because response tendency oscillates, the R with the higher average value will not always occur, because its response tendency may, at some moment, chance to be reduced more by oscillation than a competing R whose average value is less. The probability of any one response is thus an increasing function of the difference in response tendency of the competing R's and can be predicted statistically.

This survey of the Hullian system has not included several aspects which are of minor importance for the introductory purpose of this section, e.g. stimulus interaction, unlearned response tendencies, and the response threshold. We also have not shown the detail of the application of the theory. However, it is hoped that the major concepts to which we

---

of the oscillation distribution may be reduced as our knowledge and skills advance, the limit of this reduction is above zero.

shall subsequently refer have been introduced in the context which gives them their meaning.

Technical note: incentive motivation. It was stated that incentive (K) is dependent partially upon the magnitude and the time of delay of reinforcement following a response and partially upon the number of times the organism has experienced these reinforcement conditions.

Although this statement substantially reflects the Hullian position, the importance which we shall attach to this concept for predicting social behavior perhaps warrants a more detailed historical and analytical description. In the next to last version of his system, Hull postulated one variable (K) to be a function of the magnitude of reinforcement (where this magnitude is constant over trials) and another variable (J) to be a function of the delay of reinforcement, without direct reference to the learning experiences of these reinforcement conditions afforded the subject. At that time Spence suggested that these two variables could be combined and that the learning experience of the subject should be taken into account. Hull partially adopted this position in the last version of his theory and subsequently informed one of the present writers by personal communication of his acceptance of Spence's suggestion *in toto.*

According to this position, a motivated organism confronted with a primary reinforcing stimulus performs an appropriate goal response (r_G) which is isomorphic to the observable R_G, e.g. eating. Any stimulus which regularly precedes this r_G will acquire a tendency to evoke it (because the stimulus trace overlaps the r_G affording contiguity, and because the goal stimulus itself provides the reinforcement). Since the goal response cannot occur without the goal stimulus itself being present, it is hypothesized that only a portion of the r_G becomes conditioned to those stimuli preceding the goal stimulus. This portion is called the fractional anticipatory goal response (r_g), and incentive (K) is then assumed to be a function of the amplitude of r_g.

Since r_g must become conditioned to the stimuli evoking an instrumental act, the K for such a response is partially determined by the number of trials in the acquisition (or extinction) of r_g. Accordingly, incentive is itself acquired on the basis of the organism's learning experience. Further, since the magnitude of the goal stimulus will determine the amplitude of the goal response (and therefore the r_g), and since the delay of reinforcement will determine the time interval for the conditioning of r_g, the amplitude of r_g and hence K will also partially depend upon the magnitude and delay of the reinforcement.

(It may seem circular that response tendency is a function of a variable which is in turn a function of response tendency. But the incentive component of the tendency to perform the instrumental response is dependent upon tendency to perform the fractional anticipatory goal response. The latter response tendency refers to a classical conditioned response for which, according to the Spence position, no incentive variable is relevant.)

Although r_g has the status of a hypothetical intervening variable, it will perhaps be instructive to illustrate this derivation as if it were observable. If the goal stimulus is food, the goal response is eating, and we may for illustrative purposes identify the r_g as surrogate chewing responses. If we then visualize a rat running down a straight alley toward food, the incentive for this locomotion at any point on the alley will depend upon the amplitude of these surrogate chewing responses occurring at that point. These chewing responses will occur anterior to the goal end of the alley only to the extent that they have become conditioned to the cues of the alley. Each time that the rat traverses the alley and obtains food, a trial will have been afforded for this classical conditioning. But because habit requires a number of trials to reach its asymptote, the tendency to perform the surrogate chewing responses (i.e. r_g and hence K) will not reach its final level immediately. Accordingly, the incentive component of the tendency for the locomotion response will depend partially upon the number of times the subject has experienced the prevailing reinforcement conditions.

Also, those alley stimuli further from the goal will have a smaller tendency to evoke the chewing responses than will stimuli nearer the goal. This is because the tendency for a response to occur to a conditioned stimulus (in this case alley stimuli) is inversely related, except for a brief initial inversion, to the time interval between the conditioned stimulus and the unconditioned stimulus (in this case the food). (This law is derived by the theory on the basis of the stimulus trace function.) Since stimuli in the first sections of the alley are necessarily further removed in time (as well as space) from the goal stimulus than those near the goal end, the tendency for the surrogate chewing response to occur to the former will be less than to the latter. Accordingly r_g and therefore incentive (K) will be larger nearer the goal.

In this manner is derived the statement made above, that incentive (K) is dependent partially upon the magnitude and delay of the reinforcement and partially upon the number of times the organism has experienced these reinforcement conditions.

This analysis appears to work satisfactorily for a simple instrumental response such as running down an alley maze. The cues at any point in the maze become conditioned to r_g and, by evoking it,[10] provide for the K for the instrumental response. That is, the amplitude of the r_g active at any moment determines the K for the instrumental behavior at that (or the immediately succeeding) moment.

What would happen, however, if the organism were confronted with a simple choice or discrimination problem where the (two) competing responses are followed by different magnitudes (or delays) of reinforcement? To that stimulus complex which immediately precedes the choice, a greater amplitude of r_g will become conditioned on the basis of the response receiving the larger magnitude of reinforcement than on the basis of the response receiving the smaller reward. Theoretically we can separate two amplitudes of r_g conditioned to the choice stimulus complex, one appropriate amplitude from each response. But it seems logically inconsistent that two different amplitudes of the r_g can coexist; moreover, this position would require the postulation of some higher-order property in the organism capable of directing the two K's determined by the two r_g's upon the appropriate response tendencies. Let us examine possible alternatives to this description.

One could, of course, assume that the separate response tendencies summate so that a single amplitude of r_g will occur. This will provide a single K which could be held to multiply all habits in the same way that Hull provides a single D which multiplies

10. It should be noted that the evocation of r_g as a classical conditioned response does not entail a K factor.

all habits. However, while the single D notion may prove adequate, the single K notion does not appear to be useful. Each of the drives provides a characteristic drive stimulus (S_D), and when several drives are present and summate into a single D, choice behavior can depend upon the responses conditioned to each S_D. But no such characteristic stimuli can be found if the response tendencies for r_g summate to determine a single K. Because the basis for choice must be the difference in K's for the competing responses, a single K solution is inadequate.

A second alternative would argue that vacillation occurs at the choice point, that stimuli contingent upon orienting acts preceding one response evoke the r_g appropriate to that response, and that such stimuli preceding the other response evoke the appropriate r_g. For example, a rat in a T-maze looks first up one arm and gets stimuli which evoke one amplitude of r_g dependent upon the reward in that arm, and then looks up the other arm and makes the r_g appropriate to the reward on that side. In this manner, then, the two different amplitudes of r_g can be evoked at different times and could be held to set the K's corresponding to the differential reinforcements. Since the r_g's occur at different times, however, the organism must be provided with some higher-order process which will receive and store the now separated K's until a decision is reached as to which response will occur. For that matter the basic problem is only postponed by this description, for the theorist must now turn to an explanation of why the vacillation occurred in the first place. Why, that is, should a rat that has nosed into one alley and set a K and resulting response tendency to traverse that arm suddenly hold this response tendency in abeyance until it surveys the alternative responses?

While this second alternative may prove to be the most useful description, some of the writers hold a tentative preference for a third possibility which requires that the symbol K be changed to sKr in order to denote that it is specific to a particular stimulus-response connection. According to this position the sKr for any response on some trial is set by the amplitude of r_g which occurred on the preceding trial. In the choice situation the sKr's are specific to the particular responses; sKr_1 and sKr_2 at any trial are dependent upon the amplitude of r_g on the preceding occurrences of r_1 and r_2 respectively. The two sKr's then enter into the determination of the competing response tendencies.

Relation to Physiology

We have briefly described the intervening-variable approach and the system resulting from Hull's use of this method of theory construction. The intervening variables describe the hypothetical content of a model organism which yields the same input-output (S-R) relations as have been observed in the behavior of actual organisms. Thus, for example, a rat's behavior is seen to vary systematically with changes in the number of hours of deprivation of food. According to the theory, such deprivation conditions produce drive (D) inside the model organism, and changes in this drive produce variations in response tendency ($s\bar{E}r$) and hence in performance. The system is useful for predicting behavior if the model organism and the real organism yield the same S-R relation. This is the basis for such statements as: The rat behaves *as if* he had a drive produced by deprivation of food.

The relations between intervening variables in a model organism and actual physiological events in a real organism have frequently been debated. Many behavior scientists insist that an intervening variable has nothing to do with any physiological phenomenon. A more moderate statement is that an intervening variable bears a relationship to a physiological event only when the behavior scientist chooses to define the intervening variable in that way. As long as the theorist does not introduce physiological terms into his partial definitions of intervening variables, however, the physiologist cannot contribute directly to the development or verification of such a behavior theory. A physiological interpretation does not have to be given all intervening variables at once. It is possible to attempt such an interpretation of one or a few, as the behavior theorist may decide. Even this degree of coalescence between physiology and behavior theory, although an admirable aim, seems remote at present. Behavior theory as presented here does not offer the physiologist any useful research orientation until some physiological interpretation is given to intervening variables. On the other hand, any model of the organism developed by physiology must account for the actual stimulus-response relations observed in behavior. Thus behavior investigations place limits on the type of model the physiologist can offer.

As Spence has pointed out, mere labeling of intervening variables with physiological terms does not constitute an adequate interpretation of those variables. One class of intervening variables which is highly susceptible to such a casual physiological interpretation is the so-called "internal response," such as fear and r_g. Real organisms, however, do not necessarily make such responses. These internal responses are merely part of the theory, and their use in a theory does not justify their reification as an actual response by a real organism. A real organism may perform responses which could be labeled "fear" or "r_g," but until such identification is made it is gratuitous if not confusing to talk as if real organisms make them. The actual identification of these internal responses seems a physiological problem.

Within an intervening-variable theory, the use of internal responses is quite legitimate. Naturally, like any other class of terms in such a theory, they should be kept to a minimum, particularly since they have the tendency to multiply with great rapidity and since calling a term like "r_g" an internal response encourages its reification.

Intervening variables, then, are constructs that may not be explicitly related to any physiological events. The nature of these intervening variables was described in general in an earlier section of this chapter. We wish now to give somewhat more detailed and specific discussion of the nature and use of an intervening-variable system.

Quantification

In general any theory will increase in value as a vehicle for prediction as the functional relations among its variables are precisely specified. Although in many instances such precise specification appears eventually achievable, many difficulties are apt to preclude its immediate attainment. In such instances the investigator may make some use of only partial knowledge about a given functional relation, for example, some knowledge regarding the sign of the slope of such a relation or, more restrictively, some knowledge of its curvature. The use of such general knowledge requires special circumstances. For example, assume a theory of the form X(Y, Z),[11] where X is an increasing function of Y and a decreasing function of Z. In any such case, if our problem involves a simultaneous increase or decrease in the values Y and Z, no prediction can be made even as to the direction of change in X, given only ordinal information about the relations $X(\tilde{Y}, Z)$, etc.[12] This aspect of the quantification problem is all a familiar story in the social sciences. Were the Hullian theory stated directly just in terms of the observable variables in question, and thus in the form R(N, h, Wg, . . .), we could drop the whole discussion of quantification at this point, since quantification of the theory would involve no more than the usual problem of statistical estimation of the parameters in any such expression. However, the Hullian theory utilizes intervening variables, being stated generally in the form R(E), and E[H(N), D(h), K(Wg), . . .],[13] where E, H, D, K, . . . are the intervening variables we have previously mentioned.

It is the presence of these intervening variables in the formulation which creates certain unique problems for quantification. In this case, quantification involves more than the usual statistical and mathematical problems of estimating

11. In addition to those already encountered, the following terminological conventions will prove helpful in the discussion to follow:

Let X(Y) mean X is some function of Y; X(Y, Z) mean X is some function of Y and Z, etc.; and $X(\tilde{Y}, Z)$ mean X is some function of Y and Z, Y held constant.

12. We should perhaps note that much of the data input to the Hullian analysis has been obtained by making observations upon the effects of one independent variable at a time, all others held constant. There is, of course, no guarantee that data gathered by making observations upon $X(\tilde{Y}, Z)$ and upon $X(Y, \tilde{Z})$ will prove adequate to predict the results of the more general situation in which both Y and Z are allowed to vary.

13. Neglecting inhibition, oscillation, the multiplicative form of the expression, etc. These simplifications will not affect the subsequent discussion.

the parameters in an expression such as R(N, h, Wg, . . .). In addition, the quantification problem is one of a *satisfactory quantitative conceptualization* of relations such as R(E), H(N), etc.

In order to illustrate the special quantification problem confronting an intervening-variable system, let us describe a particular instance in which the model was used to yield a relatively precise prediction. This example represents work done in the psychology laboratories of the State University of Iowa under the direction of Professor K. W. Spence (see Ramond, 1954).

The problem posed in this instance was the prediction of the behavioral effects of employing a novel training procedure. Information was provided concerning the rate at which rats learned to approach and touch a bar to obtain food. The question was whether the experimenter could use this information and the theory to predict the animals' preference for one of two bars, when the training procedure insured a differential number of trials at each bar. In general, can information concerning one response measure under one set of training operations sometimes permit successful prediction of another response measure under quite a different set of training operations? We shall see that the theory did permit some such prediction.

The apparatus consisted of a small triangular-shaped box containing two retractable bars. Hungry black-hooded rats were admitted to this box from a starting alley when a door was raised; the response of touching a bar resulted in the receipt of a small pellet of food. Each bar could be illuminated separately, or both could be illuminated simultaneously; food was delivered only if the rat touched an illuminated bar. The rat, then, had to learn to enter the response chamber, approach the illuminated bar, and touch it. If both bars were illuminated he was rewarded for touching either bar. During trials when both bars were illuminated, a measure was obtained of the rat's choice or preference between them; when only one bar was illuminated the response tendency was measured by the speed with which he touched the appropriate bar.

First a group of rats was run to a single bar and the resulting learning curve was obtained. Only one bar was necessary for this part of the study, but half of the animals were run to one bar and the remaining half to the other bar in order to control for possible initial preferences. On each trial any particular rat, then, entered the response chamber and found the right bar, say, illuminated. As soon as this bar was touched, he received a pellet of food and was then removed from the apparatus to await his next trial. Three such trials were given each day.

On each trial the time required to touch the bar was measured and its reciprocal was recorded as response speed. This speed was found to increase as training continued, eventually reaching an apparent asymptote. The experimenter thus discovered the functional relationship obtaining for this type of subject in this apparatus between response speed and the ordinal number of reinforced trials. Conventional curve-fitting techniques were employed to specify this function in exact quantitative form.

Without further transformation of this empirical function one might only assume reasonable invariance in this relationship and thereby predict that a replication of the above study would yield an essentially duplicate quantitative finding. But we wish to show how a scientist could use the theory to assist in making a quantitative prediction about the outcome of the following quite *different* training procedure.

Suppose one begins again with experimentally naive, hungry, black-hooded rats, and runs them in the apparatus three trials a day. Instead of illuminating only one bar on each of these three trials for any animal, both bars are illuminated on the first trial so that the subject's preference can be recorded. Then, on the remaining two trials of each day the practice is distributed in such a way that each subject receives twice as many reinforced runs to one bar as to the other. Suppose an animal is to receive the greater number of trials per day to the right bar; on those days when he selects the left bar on the first trial, one illuminates (and thereby forces his response to) the right bar on both of the remaining two trials. Should such a subject choose the right bar on the first trial, only the left bar is illuminated on the second trial and only the right bar on the third trial.

By following this procedure the experimenter can record the per cent of trials on which one bar is chosen over the other and also insure that the one bar receives twice as many trials as the other. In the example where the right bar receives the greater number of trials, how can the theory be used to predict the relationship between the per cent choice of the right bar and the number of days of training?

The system holds that the per cent choice can be predicted from the *difference* in $s\bar{E}r$'s of the two responses, touching the right bar and touching the left bar. It is necessary, then, to calculate how this difference in $s\bar{E}r$'s will change as training is continued. To do this the separate $s\bar{E}r$'s must first be calculated.

The theory states that response speed, denoted Q, is a linear function of $s\bar{E}r$. Accordingly in this particular problem it is unnecessary to decompose $s\bar{E}r$ further into its components. In this apparatus for this type of subject $s\bar{E}r(N)$ is some linear transformation of the empirical equation found for $Q(N)$. Further, since one knows how many trials per day were given one can draw $s\bar{E}r$ as a function of days. If the change in $s\bar{E}r$ is plotted as a function of the number of *days*, it is clear that N for the right bar will be twice that for the left bar, and its $s\bar{E}r$ curve plotted against days will therefore approach its asymptote at *twice the rate* at which the $s\bar{E}r$ for the left bar approaches the same asymptote. The two curves will eventually converge and one can accordingly predict that the *difference* between them will begin at zero and at first will increase and later decrease. Further, since the $s\bar{E}r$ curve was stated exactly, the number of days at which the difference will reach its maximum, and the shape of its rise and fall, can be specified.

The theorist can therefore generate a prototype curve relating the *difference* between the $s\bar{E}r$'s for the right and left bars as a function of the number of days of training. The theory states that per cent choice of the right bar will be a function of this difference, and, further, that this function is ogival in form. One can accordingly transform the difference curve showing the curvature and point of maximum in the per cent choice curve. These predictions were confirmed.

It was impossible to predict exactly how high the per cent choice curve would go. This prediction would have required two further specifications: 1. the linear transformation of Q(N) that would provide sĒr(N) (so that the difference between the sĒr's could be specified exactly and not to a linear transformation), and 2. the size of the variance of the oscillation distribution.

Further, prediction of the results of changing some other variables (for example, the number of hours of food deprivation) would have required decomposition of the sĒr(N) curve into its components. For illustrative purposes let us show how this decomposition is accomplished.

According to the postulates of the theory, sHr is determined by the number of reinforced trials (N), K by N and the magnitude (Wg) and delay (Tg) of reinforcement, and D by the hours of food deprivation (h). The values of each of these relevant independent variables (N, Wg, Tg, and h) are known to the theorist. The sĒr's could therefore be calculated if he knew the values of the parameters of the equations relating the intervening variables (sHr, K, and D) to these independent variables. We wish to show how the empirical function Q(N) can provide some, though not all, of these parameters. Q(N) will yield the parameters of sHr(N) and K(N).

Response speed is assumed to be a linear function of sĒr; we know *post hoc* that the relationship sĒr(N) must be some linear transformation of the equation Q(N). It is presumed further that D remains constant over N, so the product (sHr x K) as a function of N must also be a linear transformation of the function Q(N). We must therefore simply decompose some linear transformation of the relation Q(N) into two equations, sHr(N) and K(N), with the restriction that the product of these latter two functions equals the one with which we began.

In this particular instance the ways in which sHr and K change with N are not independent. Since K is dependent upon the amplitude of r_g, that portion of the tendency to make r_g which changes with N is the sHr_g. Accordingly two sHr's change with N, that for the instrumental response and that for the r_g. If we add the restriction that the rate of growth of these habits is the same, we may perform a square-root transformation upon our original function Q(N), and the resulting equation then states the functions sHr(N) and K(N).[14]

In addition to illustrating the intervening-variable method of theorizing, this extensive deduction serves as a convenient stage on which to present several points regarding the quantification problem faced by Hullian theory.

1. If any statements more precise than the "greater-than" variety are to be made, certain kinds of advance information concerning the particular subspecies of subject and the given apparatus must be available in order to permit estimation of the parameters of the relevant theoretical equations. This does not mean that the intervening variables are response inferred [15] in the sense that they depend for their estimation upon the behavior to be predicted. It is true that the parameters of equations defining intervening variables can be estimated only with the aid of certain empirical data obtained from comparable subjects in a comparable apparatus. But these data can be obtained under conditions other than those about which we wish to predict, and the assumption of invariance in these theoretical equations permits prediction concerning novel conditions.

2. Whenever the species of subject or the apparatus are changed, the quantification system set up is inapplicable. For

14. This specific square-root solution is presented for illustrative purposes. It holds only when delay of reinforcement is zero and magnitude of reinforcement infinite.

15. In one sense all hypothetical terms employed by social scientists are response inferred: observations of variations in behavior suggest to the scientist that these result from variations in some state of the organism. Improved performance suggested to Hull an increase in sEr; to Tolman the formation of a "clear" sign-gestalt-expectation; to Köhler the occurrence of a "good" gestalt. Such notions become genuinely useful to some scientists, however, only after further specification is made relating sEr (sign-gestalt-expectations, or gestalts, or what you will) to some stimulus and antecedent conditions. Otherwise prediction is impossible, since their values can never be known until after the behavior in question has occurred.

the Hullian theorist the advantages of a quantified system are sufficiently great as eventually to override this handicap. Perhaps some simplifications will be discovered, e.g. inhibition may be found to increase at a constant ratio with the rate at which habit is accumulated, although the absolute values of inhibition and habit may vary.

3. We have seen that the quantification methodology generally results in decomposing some obtained function into several components meeting the restriction that they can be recomposed into the original equation by the principles of the theory. With only a single function there are an indefinitely large number of satisfactory decompositions. If, for example, one wished to decompose the function R(N) into E(N) and R(E), the second could always be satisfactorily selected on the basis of any arbitrary selection of the first function. In this case the quantification solution is trivial. Indeed, there is no guarantee that with a large number of quantitative empirical generalizations there is any solution, much less a unique one. Arriving at one solution, however, may assist the task of making exact predictions even though some other equally satisfactory solution could have been found.

4. Predictions are delivered by the system in its entirety, but it may nonetheless be possible to make relatively precise predictions on the basis of only partial quantification if some variables are held constant and do not therefore differentially affect the behavior in question.

5. The mathematical operations embodied in the theory can be applied only ordinally until exact quantification is attained. At the present time one cannot solve for values of sHr, K, and D, and perform the indicated multiplication. One can, however, make ordinal statements about changes in these variables.

6. The theory can never be stated more exactly than the empirical generalizations upon which it is based. The need for precise systematic research is therefore accentuated.

Technical note: scaled speed. One of the most industrious attempts at quantification of a theoretical model in the behavior area has been that of Hull et al. (1947) and his associates (Gladstone et al., 1947) in a series of articles on the quantification of reaction potential. This procedure involves a modification of the scaling technique introduced by Thurstone (1927, Case III). It is our opinion, however, that this particular procedure was incorrectly conceived. Hull et al. (1947, p. 253) assert that this methodology constitutes a "strict operational definition of reaction potential," a statement which, if accepted, would make reaction potential a response-inferred construct. Such a position disregards the fact that, in order to be useful, reaction potential must be calculated from stimulus and antecedent conditions. Any construct which depends for its estimation upon the behavior which it was intended to predict is simply useless.

The Hull methodology actually yields a new response measure which we might call "scaled speed." This response measure is defined by a set of operations performed upon the obtained data which is, in principle, no different from a transformation of raw data into reciprocals, per cent response, and the like. The apparent peculiar advantage of scaled speed as opposed to some other response measure is that the operations used in its calculation require that it bear a linear relationship to reaction potential. In exactly similar fashion the operations performed in calculating response probability require that this measure bear an elongated S-shaped relationship to reaction potential.

To the extent that linear functions are simpler to fit and utilize, scaled speed might have a certain usefulness. However, Hull's postulates also hold that response speed (reciprocal of latency) bears a linear relationship to reaction potential, and from this point of view alone one could hardly justify the added computational labor involved in transforming speeds into scaled speeds.

While this statement is reasonably valid, several technical errors in the Hull methodology must be noted. First, the use of this scaling method requires that latency be (and Hull there writes as if it were) a function of response tendency ($s\hat{E}r$). In his system, however, latency is determined by effective reaction potential ($s\bar{E}r$) without oscillation. Logically something which changes from moment to moment would not be appropriate for predicting a time parameter; a latency may be sufficiently long for $s\hat{E}r$ to take on a number of values before the response occurs. Indeed, latency can be predicted on the basis of the probability of a superthreshold $s\hat{E}r$ which is a function of the threshold and $s\bar{E}r$. Accordingly, the methodology simply is not appropriate to latency data, although it could be applied meaningfully to amplitude which is determined by $s\hat{E}r$.

It should be recognized that the fact above voids Hull's estimation of the shape of the oscillation distribution, since the variations in latency do not result directly from $s\hat{E}r$. However, Hull did change his system to hold that the sigma of oscillation changes during learning trials. If this is true then the methodology suffers another technical fault. For this procedure scales the means of the distributions upon which the scale is based, but $s\bar{E}r$ is the upper limit of the oscillation distribution. When the sigma of oscillation is a constant, then the mean is constantly displaced from $s\bar{E}r$ and a scale of the means is linearly related to $s\bar{E}r$. When, however, one assumes that the sigma of oscillation can vary, then the difference between this mean and $s\bar{E}r$ is not constant, and scaling the means does not provide a linear estimate of $s\bar{E}r$. The scaling procedure will be useful, therefore, only if the mean of the oscillation distribution, rather than its upper limit, is taken as $s\bar{E}r$, or if the sigma of that distribution is assumed to remain constant.

Scaled speed may have some extra value in testing more detailed deductions of a theoretical model and as such may be a useful response measure. But it in no wise alters the basic problem of quantification.

CHAPTER 3

DEFINITIONS AND PROPERTIES OF RESPONSES

IN this section we shall take up two major problems which arise in the study of responses as dependent variables in behavior science. These problems concern 1. the definition and measurement of responses, and 2. the consistency of behavior in a wide variety of situations.

Definitions of Responses

Any study using responses as dependent variables treats the actual behavior of an organism in terms of some set of categories or definitions of responses. When we discuss the response of salivation or the response of blushing, we ignore small or even large variations which characterize the actual behaviors from one instance to another. Thus the social sciences never deal with behavior per se, but rather with categories or classes of responses. The problems in studying responses are then to obtain a reliable method for their classification and, with the aid of such a method, to seek regular relations between antecedent conditions and responses. In this way reliability and fruitfulness become two standards by which one must judge a set of response definitions. Obviously these standards are related; we must also add ease of application as another. Our purpose now is to examine the reliability, ease of application, and fruitfulness of various methods which have been used in the social sciences for defining responses. We shall see that any method involves a compromise between two or all three of these standards.

Definition of responses is a double operation. An observer, whether or not he is aided by some apparatus, must combine certain concrete instances of behavior; he also must separate some instances from others. In making response definitions the observer is limited by his apparatus or his perceptual acuity; he may be further limited by his cultural and, especially, his linguistic background. Thus characteristics of the observer (and apparatus, where it is used) always impose certain ways of classifying various behaviors together and of separating still others.

Social scientists appear to approach the problem of defining responses in four different ways. First, responses have been defined exclusively in terms of movements of the organism; for example, "high front unrounded vowel" (Bloch, 1948), and "left sneer" (Birdwhistell, 1952). This type of definition will be referred to as the "movement" type. Secondly, responses have been defined with respect to some changes made in a piece of apparatus; for example, "bar depression" (Perin, 1942; Williams, 1938), and "strident" versus "mellow" sounds (Jakobson, Fant, and Halle, 1952). We shall call this the "apparatus" type of definition. A third way of defining responses has been with respect to one or more presumed direct effects, not further specified, on some organism(s) other than the one whose behavior is being categorized. As examples of this type of definition, which we shall denote the "other-organism" type, we have "realistic" versus "conventional" art styles (Herskovits, 1950, pp. 378–439), and "gives information" and "agrees" (Bales, 1950). Finally, responses have been defined with respect to some presumed internal state of affairs which the observer somehow "perceives" in the organism under study; we shall call this fourth type the "internal-state" method of defining responses; as examples, we have "shows tension" (Bales, 1950) and "cathects" (Parsons, 1951).

Two points arise from these distinctions between ways of defining responses. The first point, which is obvious from the examples taken from Bales, is that a set of response definitions may use more than one of the four types of definition. The second point concerns the interrelationships between these four methods. We shall discuss this latter point more fully, but first we must make a distinction between responses and response aggregates.

The difference between a response and a response aggregate is always relative to some set of response definitions. For example, suppose that in using the other-organism type of definition we can distinguish a number of responses. Each element in the set defines a response. Now, we can take several elements from the original set and put them into one category; this new category is then a response aggregate with respect to the original set of definitions. Counting instances of a response and obtaining rates of performance may be viewed as ways of aggregating responses, but we shall discuss these latter topics when we treat response measures. Since we shall not deal with them here as one way of aggregating responses, we will restrict the meaning of aggregation to cover only the combination of different elements of a set of response definitions. The reasons for the aggregation of certain responses are numerous; two obvious and frequent factors are convenience of application and the aims of the investigator.

The relations between the four methods of defining responses are largely those of aggregation. A single response, according to an other-organism type of definition, for example, may be translated into an aggregate of responses defined in terms of movement. Social scientists sometimes make such translations by equating responses of the internal-state or other-organism varieties to aggregates of responses defined by the apparatus and/or movement methods. Essentially this process eliminates internal-state and other-organism definitions and merely borrows labels from the first two types of methods to name aggregates composed of responses defined by movements or apparatus. Bales, for example, characterizes his response "shows tension" partly as an aggregate of movement-type responses, such as "bites fingernails" and "doodles." Although we have no *standard* set of response definitions in terms of movements or apparatus, the translation of different sets of response definitions into some based on movements or apparatus may be very helpful.

But in examining translations of other-organism or internal-state types of definitions into apparatus or movement types, we frequently find hints that the translation has not been complete. An internal-state response, such as "shows tension," will frequently be applied where the scientist cannot observe any of the responses defined by movement or apparatus, which make up the aggregate labeled "shows tension." Some undefined residue is left over and is not specified in terms of movement or apparatus criteria. This residue is a continual source of difficulty in treating responses, since its existence may prevent adequate communication of techniques or reliability of results. An investigator who cannot fully verbalize his response definitions may sometimes be able to train observers to make judgments agreeing remarkably well with his own. Apparently, along with many other factors, our natural language permits us to give rather consistent labels to cues from another person's behavior, even though we cannot explicitly identify those cues. This circumstance, however, leaves the investigator open to misinterpreting behavior or seriously distorting his observations, because of limitations imposed on him by his own culture. The danger of culture-bound ways of viewing behavior has been emphasized in the anthropological literature, and we will not repeat here what others have said on this topic. The development of a crossculturally applicable set of response definitions does not appear feasible to us as long as the usual common-sense response categories are not fully reduced to aggregates of objectively defined elements. The ways in which one aggregates such elements, however, may change from culture to culture, just as in linguistics: what are allophones of a single phoneme in one language may be independent phonemes in another.

We do not want to leave the impression that aggregation of responses is done only by taking elements from one set and relating them to elements in a second. Frequently, for example, a particular problem requires that elements in a set of response definitions be aggregated according to some criterion of efficiency or "correctness" of performance. In a problem-solving study the task may be so arranged that a few temporal sequences of responses, defined in terms of apparatus, are "correct," while all others are "incorrect." Within the aggregate "incorrect response," the experimenter also may attempt to distinguish different types, or subaggregates, of incorrect procedures. Aggregation done this way is usually determined by the particular demands of the problem and/or by the investigator's interests; it often includes temporal sequences of individual responses instead of merely involving individual responses without regard to the "context" of other responses in which they occurred. In these cases aggregation is based on a criterion or goal which the investigator sets for his subject. Furthermore, in a new experiment certain response sequences which were once aggregated as "wrong" may now be aggregated as "correct." Here, however, aggregation is still relative to some initial set of response definitions, and the reliability of the response aggregates is a function of the reliability of the initial reference set. We can now consider in more detail each of the four methods of defining responses, since this discussion turns partially on the question of aggregation, which affects the reliability, ease of application, and generality or fruitfulness of a set of response definitions.

Internal-state definitions [1] have long been popular in social science because of their apparent ease of application. Insofar as they are based on elements in a common linguistic and cultural background, they permit at least nominal communicability, even when internal-state definitions are not reduced to objective definitions. The reliability of this class of definition, however, is hampered by the fact that the personal or cultural background of the investigator using it introduces ambiguity; two investigators, for example, may easily use the category "feels guilty" in such radically different ways that one suspects their own personal backgrounds play a significant role in the application of such categories. Within a given culture, however, the chances are good that this type of definition may be reliable and fruitful. Furthermore, many social scientists feel that reductions of internal-state definitions to aggregates of movement-type or apparatus-type elements have not been adequate up to now; indeed, some

1. Though labeled somewhat similarly, so-called "internal responses" (Hull, 1943a) are quite different in logical status from internal-state definitions. These of course are not responses at all but logical constructs in a behavior theory, and are discussed in Chap. 2.

feel that such reduction can never be adequate. We do not know of any evidence which rules out for all time the adequacy of any reduction of internal-state definitions to other types. Perhaps some responses defined on the basis of internal states will never be reduced to an aggregate of elements based on criteria of apparatus or movement; to this extent, the social sciences using the former will always have an overlay of "insight." We believe, however, that such an overlay can be considerably reduced from its present size.

Considerations similar to those just outlined for internal-state definitions apply to definitions based on presumed effects of a response on another organism. Through our natural language such definitions are easily applied; but their reliability often may be low and they frequently involve the use of some insight on the part of the investigator. Similarly, such definitions often have been fruitful in the study of our own culture but are of dubious value when applied to other cultures. But even within a given culture, the use of this type of definition requires precise specification of the identity of the other organism, since effects on other organisms may differ from one individual to another. Actually other-organism definitions, instead of imputing internal states to the organism making the response, merely shift the imputation to some other organism. Finally, many attempts have been made to reduce other-organism definitions to aggregates of elements from movement-based or apparatus-based systems. Such aggregates may include movements on the part of the organism whose response is under consideration or on the part of the other organism used as the criterion for defining the response. The last case, where one studies the behavior of a second organism in order to categorize that of the first, offers one paradigm for investigating interaction.

Under the rubric "apparatus definitions" we include those definitions of responses where the investigator observes (and counts) changes in a physical manipulandum in order to decide whether or not a response has occurred. Bar pressing is a classical example of this, as are responses recorded by a variety of electromechanical methods. The investigator observes only the apparatus and need not pay direct attention to the organism itself. But the investigator presumes a high correlation between movements of the organism and movement of the apparatus. Experimental psychology has utilized this method very heavily, since it is generally reliable and permits comparisons of performance among different species. In a wide variety of situations, however, responses defined on the basis of apparatus are hard to use; furthermore, such response definitions often suppress considerable information about the subject's activity. To overcome this last difficulty the investigator often supplements recordings of responses defined by apparatus with notes on the subject's movements. Other relations between responses defined by movement and those defined by apparatus will be discussed later.

Definitions of responses based on movements have been used unsystematically and together with other types of definitions in many investigations of human behavior. For example, such definitions are used in a first description of what the investigator believes is previously unreported behavior (Herskovits, 1950; Kroeber, 1948; Kluckhohn, 1949). Attempts to formulate a rigorous systematics of response classification in linguistics have been based on movement definitions (Twaddell, 1935; Hockett, 1942; Trubetzkoy, 1939; Bloch, 1948; Harris, 1951). Following the linguistic leads, Birdwhistell (1952) has attempted the same kind of classification for nonlinguistic behavior in what he terms "kinesics." We should perhaps include here such classical conditioning responses as flexion and eye blinking.

Reliability and generality of application, at least potentially, are attractive aspects of response definitions based on movements of the organism. The success of these definitions in linguistics is quite remarkable. But a general use of such a system of response definitions would be difficult, especially in the absence of an efficient notation. Perhaps notational short cuts can be worked out, as they have been in linguistics, without losing vital information. At present we seem far from having a workable general system of movement-based definitions, and other types probably will be of more immediate use.

Interrelations between Movement and Apparatus Definitions

We previously deferred discussion of the relations between movement-based and apparatus-based definitions. These interrelationships are best brought out by considering two problems: first, the interpretation of Hull's "molar-molecular" distinction in the light of our analysis of definitions of responses, and second, the role of the environment in establishing response definition.

Hull borrowed from Tolman the notion that the task of behavioral analysis was to study "molar" behavior, although this position was later modified (Hull, 1952). The concept of molar behavior implied that interest should be centered on response phenomena which emerge from the coordinated action of many muscle groups, as against a "molecular" analysis of the action of each single group. Actually, there is no clear dividing line between molar categories and molecular ones, although discussion of this distinction has often proceeded as if a line existed. From our point of view it makes little sense to ask how molar is a given level of analysis; one can only ask whether a response defined by one criterion is an aggregate of responses defined by another. Molarity and its companion molecularity are useful concepts only in comparing *two or more* systems for defining responses. One system is more molecular than a second when the first breaks into two or more separate categories a single response category drawn from the second. Furthermore, this relationship holds only for that single case, since it may be reversed for some other response in the first system. The question of how molar behavioral analysis should be is answerable only in terms of the investigator's interests and the techniques available.

On first glance it might appear that single responses defined in terms of apparatus are generally more molar than those defined on the basis of movements. For example, a rat can press a bar in a large number of ways. But response definitions based on apparatus are not necessarily more molar relative to those based on movements, as we know from electromyography (see Gellhorn, 1953), where action potentials are recorded from individual muscles. In this case one can distinguish electrical differences between two instances of behavior that would be called the same on the basis of a movement definition. The molar-molecular distinction is not generally applicable to the relations between apparatus-based and movement-based definitions of response. The distinction may apply in either direction, depending on the apparatus used and the movements studied.

Definitions of responses based on apparatus require the organism to produce some change in the physical environment surrounding him; but some categories of responses based on movements also reflect changes in, or relations of the organism to, the physical environment. For example, we might use "turning toward the window" as a response category, although it may involve the same movements as would "turning toward the door" on another occasion. Obviously we may use spatial and temporal relations between organism and environment to break down into further categories a single response class defined by movements. The investigator usually does this in terms of the particular problem which he is studying and in terms of his particular setup. In such cases each response definition, which may have elements of both movements and apparatus, is determined prior to making observations.

Where apparatus is available to distinguish several amplitudes, for example, of a single response defined by movements, this combined technique may add both precision and cumbersomeness to the investigation. Beyond this, however, the combination of apparatus-based and movement-based criteria for defining responses raises some serious theoretical problems for a system like Hull's; we shall discuss these problems after first defining "dimensions" of a response.

Response Dimensions

Any method used for categorizing responses raises the problem of quantifying responses, which requires that the investigator decide on the dimensions of a given response which he wants to study. This problem has been discussed most frequently by psychologists, who have utilized apparatus-type definitions of responses, and has some important theoretical implications.

By "dimensions" of a response we mean the ways in which we can measure variations in that particular response. For example, suppose we have a (movement-type) response category, "raising the left arm." This response may vary in magnitude, since the arm can be raised to different heights, or in speed, or in latency, and so forth. These variations constitute the dimensions of this response. We can divide the dimensions of a response into two major types: dimensions measurable on a single instance of a response, and those measurable only on multiple instances. For example, we can measure the latency or speed of a single response, but any measure involving the frequency of a response can be obtained only by observing many instances of it. The most widely used measures of this latter type are rate, probability of response, and resistance to extinction; all these measures require observation of multiple instances of a response over time. There has recently been considerable discussion of probability of response (Skinner, 1950, for example), and it seems worth while to devote some attention to the meaning of this term.

Probability of response, which will be represented by p(R), is often used as a response dimension partly because it can be measured when only some categorization of responses is available. For example, if responses can be classified into three kinds, one can assign probabilities to each on the basis of a simple counting procedure; the probability of a response is the proportion of times which that response occurred out of the total number of responses appearing.

Unfortunately this formulation of the measurement of p(R) is only one of three types of measurement which have been discussed and used interchangeably in the literature. These three meanings of p(R) are as follows:

1. p(R) is the proportion of times a response occurs out of the total opportunities for its occurrence. This measurement assumes that the organism is operating like a stable

input-output device over time. An example of this is a trained observer in a psychophysical experiment.

2. p(R) is the proportion of a sample of different organisms showing a response at a given time. Usually all these organisms have been given the same experimental treatment, such as a fixed number of reinforced trials. Most learning curves have been drawn up in this way. Such curves are a series of points determined by the usual population-sampling techniques.

3. p(R) is a measure of the "certainty" that an organism will make a given response within a fixed amount of time. For example, we are more or less certain that a friend will reply to a letter within the next week. This type of p(R) expresses a relation between a statement about future behavior and data concerning past behavior by our friend and by similar people.

In recent studies of probability Carnap (1950) has pointed out that there are two types of probability. One is probability_1, or logical probability, which states the degree of confirmation of or certainty about a sentence on the basis of given evidence. Type C is a probability_1 measure. The other kind of probability distinguished by Carnap is probability_2, which states the relative frequency of an event for all possible occasions for the event. The p(R) measures of type A and B are probability_2 measures. Obviously measures of types A or B may contribute to the formation of a p(R) measure of type C. Probability_2 measures may sometimes serve as evidence for another statement to which a measure of degree of confirmation is assigned. Furthermore, we may make probability_1 statements about a "true" population statistic on the basis of relative frequency measures on a sample. Fisher's statistical system makes such probability_1 statements a function of the degrees of freedom of the sample.

The analysis of probability offered by Carnap indicates that we cannot identify types A and B on the one hand with C on the other. Type C measures may be generated by type A or B measures, but they may be generated by other sorts of observations as well. Furthermore, it is quite clear that type A measures and type B measures are very different. The populations sampled by each are distinct. Finally, type C measures of p(R) are needed to measure the probability of response for a single individual, when learning or extinction is occurring. The type A measure assumes a constant $probability_2$ structure for the individual's response repertoire. This assumption is meaningless in learning situations, since there is no way of operationally specifying a $probability_2$ for the response under consideration. The assumption that one can assign a $probability_2$ measure to a response which is being conditioned in a single individual leads to the conclusion that such a measure can never be directly estimated on any one trial, since only one instance of that reponse for that $probability_2$ state is available. Empirical learning curves which show type B p(R) as a function of the number of reinforcements do not necessarily describe the behavior of a single individual.

Since a given response (or set of responses) may have several dimensions, some authors raise the problem of which of those dimensions can serve as a measure of learning. In some theoretical formulations, such as Hull's, this is a critical problem. Hull (1943a) adopted the position that all dimensions of a response are measures of the degree to which the response has been attached to new stimuli, since he wrote equations linking the various dimensions to reaction potential. This position implies that dimensions of a response are always interrelated in the same way; but data on unconditioned reflexes do not support such a position (Sherrington, 1947), nor do data on human learning of "skilled" performances, where the subject must adjust the dimensions of a response to maximally effective values. Skinner (1950), therefore, has argued that many response dimensions, such as amplitude, are learnable as such and hence cannot serve as measures of learning, and concludes that probability of response is the only measure of learning.

This argument leaves several alternatives open to Hull's theory. The first is to ignore all dimensions but probability and retain reaction potential as a single final intervening variable. Another is to have separate reaction potentials for separate response dimensions; each reaction potential for a given response would be computed in a different way. A third alternative would be to retain a single reaction potential for each response and to call responses differing in any dimension different responses. The second and third alternatives would still allow prediction of several dimensions of a response. Hull actually tried out the third alternative in his last work (Hull, 1952), where he developed a so-called "micromolar" approach and treated responses of different amplitudes as separate responses.

Under either the second or third alternative a system like Hull's becomes quite complicated, especially with continued development of the micromolar approach. If responses differing in amplitude, for example, are recategorized as "separate" responses, one must compute a number of reaction potentials in order to predict amplitude of response. A mathematically simpler approach is offered by establishing separate reaction potentials for each dimension of a response. Estes (1950) has done something similar to this in his statistical theory of learning, where he computes separate probability coefficients for different response dimensions. In its present form, however, Hull's system seems either insufficient or too unwieldy. Further development of this system would seem very promising if separate reaction potentials were set up for separate dimensions of a response.

Final Note on Response Definition

The foregoing discussion indicates that definitions based on both movements and apparatus will persist in studies of behavior. Furthermore, some combined technique, using elements from both, may be developed to the point of wide and reliable applicability, although the dimensions of a response may have to be used as criteria for defining different responses. This would demand a combined technique, such as that foreshadowed by Hull, if a system such as his is to be developed further.

While there may be many attempts in the future to introduce such refinements into stimulus-response theories, other areas of social science are not likely to be immediately affected. For each area the system of response definitions used will still depend heavily on what problems are being considered. To take a trivial case, the economist studying buying practices will undoubtedly still ignore whether a consumer uses his left or right hand to extract his wallet. The total rung up by the clerk will still be the primary datum. The gaps between various social sciences may be due to the fact that unit responses for one discipline are aggregates of large numbers of response categories used by another. To the extent that this is true, formal integration can be furthered by an explicit statement of the nature of such aggregations. The value of this procedure may lie primarily in clarifying differences between "level of analysis" of various disciplines.

Consistency and Transitivity of Behavior

In common with a number of matters thus far discussed, e.g. definition and measurement of response, response dimensions, quantification, etc., those of consistency and transitivity have an important bearing upon the design of adequate observational techniques relevant to behavior theories. In a choice situation, two or more responses are available. Behavior is consistent to the degree that the response chosen on one occasion is repeated on other occasions; transitivity means that if response $\mathbf{R}_1$ is preferred to response $\mathbf{R}_2$ and $\mathbf{R}_2$ to $\mathbf{R}_3$, then $\mathbf{R}_1$ is preferred to $\mathbf{R}_3$. A discussion of these concepts is particularly relevant to one major objective of this book, namely a consideration of the relations between Hullian theory and behavior science generally, for the following two reasons:

1. Let us consider the problem of measuring $\bar{\mathrm{E}}$ (effective reaction potential) in terms of Hull's approach. In certain experimental situations, usually designed to test hypotheses on learning, the investigator begins with a so-called "experimentally naive organism." Control of the experimental situation gives him data about the learning history of the organism between the time when prediction is made and the time when the predicted behavior should occur. He evaluates

these data in the light of principles of learning and deduces a measure of strength of tendency to perform. Useful as this method may be for certain purposes, it does not seem appropriate for many human behavioral problems. It is characteristic of these problems that the learning of the organism prior to the time of prediction is immense. In principle, if we had data on the past learning history of the organism, we could evaluate these data and thereby attempt to predict subsequent behavior. In practice, however, this method is often unusable, because the learning history of the organism is too lengthy and obscure to unscramble in this fashion. We need then some other way to determine the relevant values of $\bar{E}$, at least for some initial time period. That is, given such values for some period, we might attempt to predict changes in them by the application of principles of learning to the subsequent conditions confronting the organism. One possible method for getting initial values of $\bar{E}$ is by direct observation of the choice behavior in question. However, the kind of observation which would be appropriate for this purpose depends in an important way upon whether the behavior in question can be assumed to be consistent and/or to display transitivity. Hull's theory implies an answer to these questions. Obviously, observational techniques utilized to establish the values for variables in the theory should be consonant with the implied answer.

2. More generally speaking, social scientists often attempt to establish empirical generalizations about behavior by direct observations upon the behavior about which they desire to predict. The design of any such observational technique must be based upon some assumption about the consistency and/or transitivity of the behavior in question. The Hullian theory attempts to explain why strengths of tendency to perform possess the values that they do; hence the theory makes some implications about consistency and transitivity. These implications are important to investigators of behavior whether or not they contemplate application of the Hullian analysis or any other explicit behavior theory. (Often such analysis is conducted without explicit reference to any theory

which purports to explain how the observed tendency to perform came to have a particular value.)

We may now set up our problem generally. Assume some stimulus situation which might evoke any one of the behavioral events $R_1, R_2, \ldots R_i$. Upon presentation of the stimulus, the probability that some R in the class will occur is unity. The occurrence of any R in the class precludes the occurrence of any other on that trial. The investigator attempts to predict which R will occur. This sort of problem is commonly termed "choice behavior."

In the analysis of certain behavior such problems are approached by directly establishing empirical generalizations for the choice behavior in question. In order to facilitate subsequent discussion the analysis may be described in general terms as follows: [2]

The investigator defines (in terms of certain operations) a number sequence $\bar{E}_1, \bar{E}_2, \ldots \bar{E}_i$, assigning the number $\bar{E}_i$ to the behavioral event R_i, and so on. He predicts that the R for which $\bar{E}$ is the greatest will occur.[3] A possible numbering rule for specifying $\bar{E}_1, \bar{E}_2, \ldots \bar{E}_i$ in terms of $R_1, R_2, \ldots R_i$ is this: The investigator presents the stimulus to the subject, who is constrained for purposes of observation in such a way that only R_1 or R_2 can occur. If R_1 does occur, our numbering rule is that $\bar{E}_1$ is greater than $\bar{E}_2$. Also, R_1 is said to be preferred to R_2 (R_1PR_2); this is the operational definition of preference. The procedure continues for other pairs until the number sequence $\bar{E}_1, \bar{E}_2, \ldots$

2. See Alchian (1953) for the following way of putting the matter—substantively, not terminologically. These discussions refer particularly to the so-called "preference-system" analysis of consumer behavior, although we treat the matter more generally. Also see Samuelson (1947).

3. This is the most general statement. The empirical significance of attempting to predict behavior on the basis of this postulate of course depends entirely upon the kind of observations from which the $\bar{E}$ values have been inferred. For example, in the case of the numbering rule suggested in the text immediately following, the significance of predicting with this postulate is evidently little more than that the subject will behave at the time the predicted behavior is expected to occur as he did at the time observations of that behavior were made. In preference-analysis terminology, call $\bar{E}_1, \bar{E}_2, \ldots \bar{E}_i$ the preference function, and any set of the R's in $R_1, R_2, \ldots R_i$ the opportunity function.

$\bar{E}_i$ has been specified. A simple example will illustrate the measurement procedure. Suppose that R_1, R_2, and R_3 are the only behavioral events possible. Observation reveals R_1PR_2 and R_2PR_3. We specify $\bar{E}_1$, $\bar{E}_2$, an $\bar{E}_3$ as, say, 3, 2, and 1 respectively. $\bar{E}$ is measured only up to a monotonic transformation. That is, any other number sequence, e.g. 9, 7, 5 respectively, in which ranking is preserved, will do as well.

When conceptualizing the measurement of $\bar{E}$ in this way, we assume that:

1. The choice behavior in question is consistent in the usual sense. That is, if we find R_1PR_2, choice behavior is completely consistent, barring new learning, if the probability of a repetition of this event after another presentation of the stimulus is unity.

2. The behavior displays transitivity. This will be the case if R_1PR_2 and R_2PR_3 imply R_1PR_3.

The validity of these two restrictions has several consequences for the observational technique under discussion. If choice behavior is not consistent in the first sense, then we must give $\bar{E}_1$, $\bar{E}_2$, . . . $\bar{E}_i$ some sort of probabilistic interpretation.[4] Likewise, even if choice behavior is consistent in that sense but does not display transitivity, our numbering rule still will not uniquely specify $\bar{E}_1$, $\bar{E}_2$, . . . $\bar{E}_i$. Returning to our paradigm, let us define the opportunity function as the subset of R's in R_1, R_2, . . . R_i which the subject is allowed to make. Suppose that observation reveals R_1PR_2, R_2PR_3, and R_3PR_1. We could no longer specify values of $\bar{E}_1$, $\bar{E}_2$, and $\bar{E}_3$ as, e.g. 3, 2, and 1 respectively. For, with nontransitivity of choice behavior, the value of $\bar{E}_1$ depends upon the particular opportunity function in which R_1 appears. This is very important for potential economy of observation. Let us take the events R_1, R_2, . . . R_{10}. We often wish to predict changes in choice behavior following changes in the opportunity function. In this choice situation there are many possible opportunity functions; there are forty-five possible pairs alone. If it is a legitimate assumption

4. As Duesenberry (1949, p. 12) has pointed out in another context this would not be too serious so long as the choice behavior had a strong central tendency with only a small random component.

that choice behavior is consistent and transitive, we could specify uniquely $\bar{E}_1$, $\bar{E}_2$, $\bar{E}_{10}$ on the basis of only nine paired comparisons.[5] From then on we could predict R regardless of the opportunity function met in the future. But if choice behavior is not transitive we would have to make observations on every subset of R's in order to predict successfully which R of any subset would occur.

In Hull's analysis of choice behavior he postulated that that R will occur for which $\hat{E}$ is the greatest. We might observe R_1PR_2 at one time and R_2PR_1 at another because of a change in learning or in the conditions of performance; such changes are reflected in D, H, K, or I, in Hull's terms, and are not relevant to the narrower problem of consistency discussed here. (In other commonly employed terminology, such changes would be said to be reflected in a change in "tastes.") Inconsistency may arise from behavioral oscillation (sOr) even when all other intervening variables are said to be constant; we are concerned with this latter problem.

The sOr postulate says that the value of $\hat{E}$ associated with any given value of $\bar{E}$ will be randomly distributed about the value of $\bar{E}$. This postulate implies that some choice behavior will be inconsistent.[6] Suppose that R_1 and R_2 constitute the opportunity function. If p is the probability of the event R_1PR_2, then 1-p is the probability of the event R_2PR_1. The

5. This would happen only if we were fortunate enough to select the observational pairs in order of preference (Alchian, 1953).

6. Data suggesting this postulate are these. If a group of subjects is run under conditions where all parameters of learning (i.e. of the subjects and the environment) known to be relevant are held constant, there is still some unexplained variance in the relation between performance and number of reinforced trials. Part of the variance is explained on grounds of individual differences between subjects; this cannot be eliminated by even the most careful selection of members comprising the group. Part of the variance, however, is held to be due to oscillation (sOr) on the part of each organism. It is postulated that even if one subject were run many times under conditions where learning status did not vary (i.e. where $\bar{E}$ retained its original value), there would still be some unexplained variance. One could, of course, question the legitimacy of "explaining" unexplained variance by postulating a random construct for the purpose. For the present, the issue of the legitimacy of sOr doesn't make much difference, since in the present state of development of the theory our predictions will be subject to some probabilistic interpretation. From the long-run point of view, the postulation of sOr really amounts to asserting that this will always be the case.

magnitude of p depends upon the relative levels of $\bar{E}_1$ and $\bar{E}_2$ and upon the deviation of $\dot{E}$ on any trial due to sOr. If we had these latter values, we could calculate p. (In the special case where $\bar{E}_1$ equals $\bar{E}_2$, we would expect p to equal .5 on the basis of this information alone.) In general, as $\bar{E}_1$ grows larger relative to $\bar{E}_2$, R_1 becomes more probable and p can equal 1. Thus some choice behavior may be completely consistent. The Hullian formulation suggests that we cannot generalize about the consistency of choice behavior from information about a particular case of choice behavior. Each case may be different.

The Hullian theory does imply that choice behavior is transitive,[7] that is, the theory concerning the constitution of $\bar{E}$ values is such that if $\bar{E}_1$ is greater than $\bar{E}_2$ and $\bar{E}_2$ greater than $\bar{E}_3$, then, barring additional learning, $\bar{E}_1$ is necessarily greater than $\bar{E}_3$. Of course, if choice behavior is not also consistent, we must use some probability interpretation of transitivity and may thereby lose a good bit of the predictive power that might possibly be derived from this characteristic of behavior.

Suppose that adequate techniques reveal that $p(R_1PR_2)$ was, say, .6. In this case Hull's theory does imply that if $p(R_1)$ is greater than $p(R_2)$ and $p(R_2)$ greater than $p(R_3)$ then $p(R_1)$ is necessarily greater than $p(R_3)$. But in such a case we can no longer predict the outcome of single trials with much assurance of success. (We discussed earlier in this chapter the probability measures relevant for a single trial.) Now the theory suggests that we make this kind of prediction: given X presentations of S_i, R_1 will occur .6X times and R_2 will occur .4X times. If we viewed our problem as one of predicting the outcome of a single trial, our number rule would be this: if $p(R_1PR_2)$ is greater than .5, $\bar{E}_1$ is

7. The basic explanation for transitivity as a characteristic of choice behavior seems to lie in the circumstance of the preference function being independent of the particular opportunity function in question, once learning is complete. In consequence, transitivity might not be implied by Hullian-type formulations which make inhibition (the negative component of tendency to perform) some function of the alternative in the opportunity function. An example is the Dollard-Miller double-approach-avoidance model (Dollard and Miller, 1950).

greater than $\hat{E}_2$. But where the probabilities of competing responses are near .5, it is not very fruitful to treat the problem in terms of an ordinal sequence $\bar{E}_1, \bar{E}_2, \ldots \bar{E}_i$ designed to predict the outcome of single trials. Rather, the theory suggests establishing a new number sequence G_i which would be related to the old sequence. In the old sequence $\bar{E}_i$ refers to R_i, but in the new one G_i refers to the proportion of times R_i is made. Our numbering rule now says that if $p(R_1PR_2)$ is .6, G_1 is .6 and G_2 is .4.[8] Unlike $\bar{E}_i$, G_i is measured in a cardinal sense. This last point raises problems about application of the transitivity assumption to allow observational economy. If $p(R_1PR_2)$ is .7 and $p(R_2PR_3)$ .7, we can predict from Hull's system the value of $p(R_1PR_3)$ if we know the standard deviations of $\hat{E}_1$, $\hat{E}_2$, and $\hat{E}_3$. With an ordinal sequence of $\bar{E}_i$'s, when we have information showing R_1PR_2, $R_2PR_3, \ldots R_9PR_{10}$, we can immediately infer R_1PR_{10} without ever having made an observation on the pair R_1 and R_{10}. In the case of a cardinal sequence, our information shows $p(R_1PR_2)$, $p(R_2PR_3), \ldots p(R_9PR_{10})$. Now, inferring $p(R_1PR_{10})$ would demand considerable calculation and considerable cumulative error. It might be easier to get that information by direct observation upon the pair R_1 and R_{10}.

Finally, it should be pointed out that in the special case in which we had reason to believe that the choice behavior in question was very nearly consistent, we could proceed with the earlier numbering rule and utilize the transitivity postulate to achieve any possible economy of observation. In this case our interpretation of $\bar{E}_1, \bar{E}_2, \ldots \bar{E}_i$ would be probabilistic only in the sense that our numbering rule involved some small random error.

8. As we noted above, probability of response is often used as an index of strength of tendency to perform. This would seem to be inappropriate in choice situations. A statement about probability of response is, essentially, a statement about the joint frequency distribution of two (or more) tendencies to perform. In consequence it does not seem an appropriate dimension to measure the "strength" of any one tendency to perform.

CHAPTER 4

STIMULUS AND ANTECEDENT CONDITIONS

OUR last chapter discussed attempts to define or categorize responses, and some implications of those attempts for Hull's theory. This chapter will treat the complementary problems of identifying and measuring antecedent conditions of behavior. Since the stimulus-response analysis proposes to predict behavior from a knowledge of antecedent events or conditions, we must consider how much and what kind of information seems necessary for a behavioral approach to the social sciences. The usefulness of a stimulus-response analysis or of a theory like Hull's depends partly on how easily the antecedent conditions which affect human behavior can be measured.

Experimental psychologists have spent much time on the problems of measuring antecedent conditions; they have accumulated considerable knowledge and experience which is potentially important for a general analysis of human behavior. In this chapter we shall utilize relatively simple and precise data yielded by experimental psychology as a basis for discussing those antecedent conditions which other social sciences indicate are extremely important in the study of human behavior. This chapter is divided into three parts, entitled respectively "Stimulus Equivalence," "Motivation," and "History of Reinforcements." Before proceeding to a detailed consideration of these topics, we shall indicate briefly why each seems important.

Social scientists often stress man's abilities to generalize, to transfer behavior from one situation to another, and to solve problems. Although an analysis of these abilities must include the consideration of language, we shall delay this until the next chapter since language involves a wide range of problems in itself. Other factors also help to determine the capacities just mentioned. Human behavior varies with perception of similarities and differences in a wide variety of concrete situations; furthermore, this perception may change with experience in those situations. These latter factors fall under the topic of stimulus equivalence, the first of the three we shall review.

Motivation and history of reinforcements receive considerable attention in anthropology, sociology, and psychiatry. Many theories of human behavior concern the origin, variety, and the action of human motives, and these theories deal with the effects of satisfaction or frustration of these motives. In our terms these effects involve the history of reinforcements. Long debates over "rationality" and "irrationality," "heredity" and "environment" often center around the subjects of motivation and reinforcement. Although insufficient to arbitrate these contests, experimental data may be able to clarify them. Identification and measurement of motivation and the history of reinforcements are therefore critical to social sciences and to a stimulus-response analysis of human behavior.

Stimulus Equivalence

The immediate external environment facing an organism may vary in many respects from one occasion to another. Despite such variations the organism often makes the same response in different situations. This fact will decrease the difficulties of predicting behavior provided we know 1. the extent to which the present situation varies from past situations, 2. the behavior of the organism in these previous situations, and 3. the relations between the degree of similarity of past to present situations and the probability of repetition of a previous response. The measurement of similarity between different environments, which is our first requirement, concerned experimental psychology from its very inception. This measurement always demands that any environment be resolved into stimulus elements or classes. For example, in a simple visual test we distinguish between the "radiant stimulus," such as a flash of light, and the "rest of the environment." Beyond this it may involve stating quantitative differences between the "same" stimulus elements occurring in two different environments. On two different occasions we may assign different intensity measures to the radiant stimulus, and this assignment establishes a further classification.

We find that, historically, psychologists and others have used three methods of defining or classifying stimuli. The first resembles apparatus-based definitions of responses and involves the use of physical instrumentation and a space-time framework for classifying stimuli. Much of classical psychophysics depends on physical terminology and measurements for specifying stimuli. In principle any environment could be treated exhaustively this way, but this rarely is done since usually it would be an extremely tedious procedure. Even in psychophysics we often find exact measurements of the variable stimulus alone, and less precise statements regarding other "constant" aspects of the environment.

A second method for specifying stimuli is through the use of the investigator's natural language. The expressions "black cards," "nonsense syllables," and "loud noises" abound in the literature on behavior. These stimuli often are not further identified, or if they are it is only by the addition of a few physical details. Naturally the investigator's past history and training affect the precision and communicability of this method. This method is easily applied, particularly in the absence of expensive apparatus, and replicability is often allowed. Our natural language thus provides a way of breaking up environments into comparable elements which may be experimentally useful.

The third method of classifying stimuli actually aggregates elements derived from either of the two methods just described. An organism is exposed to a variety of stimuli; those to which he makes the same response or ones which he calls the same are put in one category, while those to which he responds differentially are placed in different categories. A variant of this is the use of response dimensions such as amplitude and frequency to establish a quantitative order among stimuli. This method is characteristic of psychophysics and many behavioral studies of stimulus equivalence. Psychophysicists sometimes assume that the response system used by the subject is a one-to-one reflection of a "true" psychological scale or order of the stimuli. A similar assumption occurs in studies of generalization and equivalence. But both types of investigation may be designated "behavioral methods" since they use some responses by a subject to aggregate stimulus elements defined by another method. The aggregation may differ with the subject or response system utilized.

Behavioral methods for aggregating stimuli therefore may depend somewhat on the subject's past experience. In psychophysics this past history is controlled by using trained observers; but in the usual tests for equivalence of stimuli the investigator deliberately establishes a stimulus-response relation first and then systematically varies stimulus conditions. These latter tests provide some explicit information about the past history of the response system acting as an indicator, although the information is usually incomplete. Psychologists often have assumed that the subject's past history influences stimulus generalization to only a minor degree. If this assumption is unjustified, however, behavioral methods of aggregating stimuli must be used in extending stimulus-response analysis to social phenomena, since these methods are sensitive to the subject's past experience. And if this assumption is unjustified, the range of generality of many behavioral "laws" may be seriously reduced. Because of the possible importance of behavioral methods of specifying stimuli, we shall briefly examine some data from the former and their theoretical implications.

Results obtained from studies of stimulus equivalence fall into two classes, those derived from single stimulus presentations and those from simultaneous stimulus presentations. The single-presentation method yields two general findings. The first is that a response conditioned to one stimulus also tends to occur to stimuli which differ from it along some physical dimension such as intensity. The greater the difference along such a dimension, the weaker is the tendency for the response to occur, a phenomenon called the "generalization gradient" (Hovland, 1937). The second general finding is that a response conditioned to one stimulus composed of several elements also tends to occur to another stimulus complex containing some of those elements. The degree of this generalized response tendency becomes greater as the number of common elements increases (Hull, 1939, 1945). In the experiments just mentioned, the investigator must show that the response will not occur to the second or test stimulus without having been conditioned to the training stimulus; in other words, he must demonstrate that there is no pre-experimental tendency for the response to occur to the test stimulus.

Given these controls, however, we may ask how a theory of behavior will predict the phenomenon of generalization between stimuli sharing common elements or those differing along some dimension. This is not so simple a problem as it might appear. It is insufficient to postulate that habits conditioned to one stimulus generalize to other stimuli in proportion to their similarity. The theory must specify this degree of similarity in advance, since exact prediction is impossible otherwise. With stimuli which are relatively easy to order physically or psychophysically, exact specification might be achieved by basing the theoretical constructs on empirical measurements of generalization. This procedure, however, restricts further predictions to the organism or class of organisms providing the initial data. And empirical generalization gradients are easily affected by differential reinforcement of responses to the stimuli on the gradient. For some investigations, however, we may need only general statements such as "The less the difference in stimulus intensity, the greater will be the similarity between stimuli," though occasionally "similarity" measured by generalization techniques is not even a monotonic function of physical difference between stimuli.

When we turn to situations in which complex stimuli, such as other individuals, appear, a theorist is unable to order these stimuli on multiple scales of many characteristics. One major problem confronting any general theory is to identify the stimuli relevant to the theory so that measures of similarity among them can be made and used in further development of the theory. Some early work in this area, for example, studied how Negroes in Chicago rank each other as stimuli according to skin color (Warner, Junker, and Adams, 1941). Much work remains, however, before we can feel secure about application of any postulate on stimulus generalization.

Similar problems arise from results obtained with the method of simultaneous stimulus presentation. In these studies the subject is presented with a pair of stimuli. Response to the positive stimulus is reinforced while response to the negative one is nonreinforced. This differential reinforcement usually results in a discrimination where the response occurs more frequently to the positive stimulus; in line with the simple generalization findings described first, this discrimination learning becomes easier as the similarity between the two stimuli decreases (Lashley, 1938).

If the subject is presented with a new pair of stimuli following this discrimination training, he may show consistent preference for one of the new stimuli. For example, if the original discrimination is between two squares differing in size, and the larger is positive, the subject tends to select the larger of an entirely new pair of squares. This phenomenon, which is called transposition (Ehrenfreund, 1952), raises a problem concerning the stimulus characteristics to which the organism responds. On one side is the absolute view that the subject learns to respond positively to the reinforced stimulus and not to respond to the nonreinforced stimulus; on the other side stands the relational view that the subject compares the two stimuli and responds to some abstracted feature such as "larger."

This problem must be settled experimentally but we can here mention only a few representative data. For the absolute view, Spence (1936, 1937) has shown that his theory of discrimination learning correctly predicts most transposition phenomena obtained with stimuli varying along some single dimension such as size or brightness. He correctly predicts that sometimes transposition will not occur or its reverse will occur; i.e. selection of the smaller of test stimuli, whereas original training had reinforced the larger of a pair. These findings frequently embarrass the relational view.

Klüver (1933), however, found that transposition may occur to test stimuli which cannot be placed on any particular dimension with the training stimuli. For example, a subject trained to select the larger of two black squares later may choose a large red circle rather than a small blue triangle. Klüver's use of the method of equivalent stimuli yielded many similar instances which favor the relational view.

At first sight, debates over the absolute and relational theories seem to concern psychologists alone. But these theories have definite implications for social scientists interested in choice behavior. In Chapter 3 we discussed the problems of the consistency and transitivity of choice behavior. The relational and absolute views each make different predictions about the conditions under which transitivity occurs. The latter, as we said, does not predict transitivity in some instances where the former does. Furthermore, proponents of each view have emphasized somewhat different variables which affect the relations between stimuli and choice behavior. Champions of the absolute view have stressed possible effects of learning on discrimination, while representatives of the relational view have favored biologically determined organizational factors in the nervous system as determining discrimination. Each side, of course, admits that variables advanced by the other do have *some* effect. Recent studies provide suggestive data on effects of past experience in choice reactions, and these have given rise to some new theoretical notions. In view of their implications for the mechanisms of choice behavior we shall briefly review these data and the concepts generated through them.

Contemporary discussions as to the way in which learning affects stimulus equivalence center on response-produced cues, which are prominent in speculation regarding the "acquired distinctiveness" of cues. The mammalian neuromuscular system contains mechanisms insuring that various responses produce stimuli which play back into the central nervous system. Some of these stimuli are called "proprioceptive" (Ruch, in Stevens, 1950) and play an essential role in behavior. We do not understand completely the mechanism by which these stimuli arise and modulate behavior, but both clinical and experimental data (Grinker, 1951) show the importance of response-produced stimuli. Besides proprioceptive stimuli other types of stimulation following effector activity are also available. For example, we hear ourselves speak, feel ourselves sit down on a hard surface, or see our fingers operating more or less accurately on a piano keyboard. Many nonproprioceptive stimuli are very important for determining further behavior. Thus any response of skeletal musculature produces marked changes in the stimuli confronting an organism.

Theoretically all these response-produced cues can serve as stimuli for further responses. Such cues, which the investigator does not directly observe, are often invoked to account for behavior which is otherwise difficult to explain. Response-produced cues and their role in behavior need further study before we can claim that new responses can be conditioned to all of them. Nevertheless these cues appear in some accounts of the phenomenon of acquired distinctiveness of cues. An example of this phenomenon comes from an experiment by Kurtz (1953), where subjects learned different motor responses to visual patterns more easily if they first had learned different verbal responses to the same stimuli. In this way it was found that attachment of one set of discriminatory responses to some stimuli can facilitate the subsequent attachment of an entirely different set of discriminatory responses to those stimuli.[1] Although three accounts are proposed for this fact, they are compatible with one another and all may be necessary to describe the empirical findings completely.

Spence (1940), in explaining this phenomenon, has offered the notion of a receptor-orienting act, like fixation of the eyes. Stimuli initially may strike receptor organs in some inefficient fashion; for example, visual stimuli which the experimenter wishes the subject to discriminate may fall on the periphery of the retina. During the first stages of

1. We shall not separately treat what is called the "acquired similarity" of cues. The reader should also be aware, however, that the learning of the same response to a pair of stimuli may retard a subsequent discrimination between those stimuli when a second response is necessary (Birge, 1941).

discrimination learning the subject may learn to orient his eyes and fixate the stimuli so as to provide optimal stimulation. This learning to orient receptors will facilitate subsequent discriminations by insuring immediate optimal stimulation when new stimulus objects are presented.

Dollard and Miller (1950, pp. 101–3), accept the receptor-orienting theory but argue that a further basis for acquired distinctiveness occurs in some situations. Suppose the first discrimination involves the learning of different verbal responses, or any other responses which are compatible with those to be learned later to the two stimuli. Dollard and Miller say that these stimuli will acquire distinctiveness, because on subsequent presentation the different verbal responses will occur and will provide response-produced cues. These cues presumably are different, and the total stimulus complex including them will be more distinctive. For example, two squares become more distinctive if the subject labels one "larger" and the other "smaller," because these verbal responses provide additional differential cues. Both the first theory described and this analysis do not argue that the original proximal stimuli as such are made more distinctive; these theories only say that the stimulus complexes are changed by cue-producing responses.[2]

The third explanation for acquired distinctiveness of cues postulates a perceptual response mediating between external stimulus events and hypothetical internal stimulus traces. We have mentioned that Hull assumed that the onset of a stimulus (S) sets up a stimulus trace (s) within his model organism. Now, some workers posit a hypothetical perceptual response (r_p) and hold that the stimulus trace is produced by this response r_p. The reception sequence then runs S-r_p-s, and the theorist may assign to r_p whatever properties he chooses. This notion is generally consistent with results obtained by Riesen (1947), which suggest that relatively sim-

2. This expression does not imply that only certain responses produce cues; most, if not all, responses provide stimuli, although the distinctiveness of these stimuli presumably varies. But certain responses, such as some linguistic ones, may have little function besides providing self-stimulation, for which Hull (1930) suggested the label "pure stimulus acts."

ple discriminations, such as those between patterns, somehow depend upon practice and are not inborn.

The perceptual response is said to be modifiable by learning, and acquisition of a discrimination between two stimuli also may involve acquiring perceptual responses which change the stimulus trace but not the proximal stimulus. Learning principles applicable to the perceptual response might duplicate those for instrumental response learning. Reinforcement of the perceptual response could be produced by reward for subsequent instrumental behavior. Perceptual learning, however, may follow unique principles, such as some suggested in the Gestalt school's work (Köhler, 1947).

Current emphasis on the role of learning in the phenomena of stimulus equivalence also has produced theories, like Hebb's (1949), which claim that relatively simple visual discriminations are learned. The general tenor of modern psychology stresses the subject's past experience as a determinant of stimulus similarity. If these ideas are correct, behavioral methods for aggregating stimuli into classes of similar and dissimilar elements will become increasingly important. And either the absolute approach to choice behavior or revised relational theories will be needed for general analysis of such behavior. Finally, such developments could produce dramatic changes in much psychological theory. These current trends may provide a stimulus-response analysis which is useful for a variety of problems in social science. We may note that some psychologists seem headed back to a position close to one held by a pioneer of experimental psychology, E. H. Weber (1846).

Motivation

So far we have concentrated on problems of measuring or specifying the immediate environmental conditions which confront the organism. Besides the external environment, a second set of conditions precedes and influences the likelihood of a response. These conditions are summed up in the term "motivation," which has been the subject of heated discussion in the social sciences. Admittedly "motivation" is a vague term and there are no hard and fast lines between discussions of motivation and those concerned with stimulus conditions and reinforcement. Most references to motivation concern internal states or internal conditions imputed to organisms in an effort to explain many aspects of behavior. For predictive purposes, however, these internal states are usually referred back to some observable circumstances in the past which may have obtained over long periods of time and which are said to be the cause of the internal states. In a theory like Hull's, reinforcement is closely linked to motivation, and knowledge about motivation is necessary for the prediction of the future effects of a reinforcement. The relations between reinforcement and motivation will be explored later in this chapter; we shall now examine a concern of many social scientists, the nature and number of motives.

Many scientists who deal broadly with human or animal behavior offer diverse lists of motives under such terms as "instincts," "wishes," "impulses," "needs," and "urges." The enumeration of drives or motives has involved three different criteria which have been used loosely, and in combination, to distinguish them. One involves separating drives according to different terminal responses, such as drinking, orgasm, fighting, fleeing, etc. This criterion often produces ex post facto explanations of terminal behavior itself as the result of a postulated motive, and it tends to gloss over problems of predicting that behavior. Secondly, conditions of deprivation or stimulation, such as lack of food or water or presence of pain, provide a criterion which allows the prediction of future behavior by correlating those conditions with future responses. Finally, motives have been distinguished according to different goal objects, such as food, money, or social prestige. This criterion differs somewhat from the first one. In defining a terminal response, some goal object like food may or may not be mentioned, but a specific behavior must be stated. If motives are distinguished according to goal objects, no observation of any specific response is necessary. Furthermore, with this final criterion the separation of motives may be based on data obtained from interrogating a subject. Thus separate motives can be determined before the subsequently predicted behavior occurs.

Each of these three methods for differentiating motives has its own peculiar difficulties. The use of terminal behavior returns us to the problems of defining responses which were discussed in Chapter 3. Use of conditions of deprivation or stimulation presents the same problems discussed in the first part of this chapter. We will not repeat the points already made regarding these two criteria but will examine further the goal-objects criterion.

The profit-maximization postulate as utilized in the conventional economic theory of the firm is an outstanding example of a motive defined by a goal object.[3] Given this postulate, we may at least formally use it in deducing a number of theorems about the economic behavior of the firm. (For example, we may deduce that, given certain cost functions, a firm will decrease its equilibrium rate of output in response to an increase in a per unit tax on its output.) The fact that the maximization type of motivation postulate at least puts definite restrictions on a theory in part accounts for its continued popularity despite extensive criticism.[4] However, the conventional use of the profit-maximization postulate in descriptive economics amounts to an attempt to infer directly certain aspects of a subject's problem-solving behavior from presumed knowledge of the problem he confronts. Such an attempt is based upon an assumption in addition to that about the subject's motivation. The additional assumption, usually neglected or implicit, is that the subject has learned the same route to the goal which the investigator deems cor-

3. Some writers seem to view this postulate as being one directly upon economic behavior (i.e. that the firm does in point of fact maximize profit) rather than as one on motive (i.e. that the firm has profit maximization as a goal or objective). Most usage, however, treats it as a motivation postulate. This postulate has been the subject of much critical discussion in the literature. In what follows, we make no attempt to review the discussion generally; rather, we discuss only one aspect of this postulate.

4. Many other goal-object motivation postulates do not share this important formal property. This will be the case where there is no agreed-upon standard route to the goal postulated. There is such agreement in the case of maximization postulates, at least if the problem is sufficiently simplified (e.g. to rule out uncertainty, etc.).

rect. This last assumption cannot be demonstrated a priori, but it may be plausible when the subject and the investigator have a common learning history.

Motivational postulates play a different role in stimulus-response analysis than in economic theory and similar structures. In the former, behavior is not inferred directly from statements about motivation. Such statements merely put broad conditions on the possible effectiveness of reinforcing stimuli, whatever the subject's behavior may be. For example, food is an effective reinforcement for any behavior only when the subject has been deprived of it for some time.

Even within psychology, however, definitions of motives based on goal objects are easy to find. This type of definition produces a rapid proliferation of motives, since one can find innumerable goal objects. Concepts such as secondary reinforcement and acquired drive tend to check this proliferation. Secondary reinforcement implies that many stimuli become goal objects through temporal association with one or more "basic" goal objects, the latter being the only ones used to define different motives. The concept of acquired drive traces a subject's attempts to obtain a goal object back to his previous learning, where, for example, acquisition of the goal object was associated with reduction in fear. This concept also states that fear, which is considered a fundamental motive, is a response which can be conditioned to external stimuli. Although these techniques reduce the number of basic motives, they do not tell how to differentiate them; nor do they prevent reification of drives like fear as some actual internal physiological response by the organism. Mowrer (1950), for example, considers fear to be an autonomic response following a painful stimulus. Since many musculoglandular events follow a painful stimulus, this identification of autonomic responses with fear rests on an undefined method for analyzing responses, and may hinder the observation of many important behavioral changes following pain.

In the history of the social sciences, numerous accounts of motivation have been suggested. These accounts have been based on one or more of the three criteria for distinguishing motives. Perhaps one difficulty in this area has been the inconsistency of these criteria. From the point of view of predicting behavior, however, any theory of motivation must specify the conditions obtaining before actual performance which generate motivation. The effectiveness of a given reinforcement depends on those conditions of deprivation or stimulation; the mere knowledge of the occurrence of reinforcement is insufficient for predictions of certain aspects of behavior. This relationship between reinforcement and motivation encourages the separation of drives on the basis of goal objects or goal responses. And since this type of separation rapidly yields an infinity of motives, social scientists, in order to make efficient predictions, are forced back to studying conditions prerequisite to the effectiveness of a reinforcement. Thus problems of specifying motivation involve the idea of reinforcement, which we shall discuss next.

Reinforcement

The law of effect has long been recognized, and Thorndike's statement introducing it into the social sciences is only one of its many formulations. Briefly this law says that when certain events (reinforcements) follow a response, the likelihood of that response in similar circumstances increases; when other events (nonreinforcements) follow the response, its likelihood of repetition decreases. If we could identify reinforcers and nonreinforcers and trace their effects on further behavior, we obviously would have a powerful tool for predicting behavior. Our previous discussion of motivation leads to the consideration of some implications of reinforcement for the analysis of human behavior. But before treating the effects of a sequence of reinforcements and nonreinforcements we shall deal with operational and theoretical problems of identifying a reinforcement.

Spence (in Stone, 1951) points out that three types of notions are involved in identifying a reinforcement: 1. the empirical law of effect, which says that certain stimuli such as food or water, under certain conditions of deprivation, will increase the probability of any response which they follow; 2. a general statement of the presumed effects of reinforcement; and 3. specific summary statements as to the exact reinforcement. Under the second type come statements such as "reinforcement increases the strength of an S-R connection," while statements under the third type specify reinforcement as drive-reduction (Dollard and Miller, 1950, p. 40) or goal response R_G. Obviously one can accept statements under the first type of notion without commitment to a particular position under the other two. An operational definition, such as the first, is obviously necessary for predicting behavior from data on reinforcement. The other two treatments of reinforcement initially rely on the operational one and suggest particular kinds of processes which follow the presentation of a reinforcing stimulus.

Identification of reinforcing stimuli therefore involves the empirical discovery of stimuli which increase the probability of response. We already know of many stimuli which possess reinforcing value for humans; undoubtedly there are still others. Empirical determination of reinforcers is useful for predicting behavior under only one of two conditions: 1. the stimulus must retain its reinforcing properties beyond the situation(s) yielding the initial observations, or 2. the loss or gain of reinforcing properties in new situations must be predictable. Secondary reinforcers are stimuli which acquire the capacity to change probability of response by being presented along with a previously reinforcing stimulus. They lose this capacity if the pairing does not occur often enough. Unless we know the history of an organism and the degree of intraspecies variability in behavior, it might be difficult to identify secondary reinforcers and to determine their probable future strength. But instead of endeavoring to present a complete catalogue of reinforcing stimuli, we first might try to discover the more stable reinforcers and see how wide a range of behavior they control. This could be done by assuming that stimuli which are reinforcing to all members of a society or one of its subgroups are very stable and powerful determinants of an individual's behavior. This assumption is plausible, since the social control of behavior demands stable reinforcers of high effectiveness and widespread usefulness. Ethnographic material thus may supply valuable information about reinforcers and may lessen the necessity for prolonged study of a single individual.

The definition of a reinforcing stimulus as one which increases the probability of response which it follows categorizes all stimuli as reinforcers or nonreinforcers. The classification of any stimulus may vary for an individual or a group over time, since secondary reinforcers may be developed or extinguished. It will also vary between different sets of people. Furthermore, within these limitations one must decide on how to treat punishment.

Punishing stimuli are defined usually as those which an organism avoids or will learn to avoid by making a response that eliminates the stimuli. This definition tells us about responses that follow the punishing stimulus. Our definition of reinforcement, however, concerns responses which *precede* a stimulus. If we try to define punishment in terms of effects on preceding responses, we find that punishment may either increase or decrease the probability of a response. When the response which follows punishment is the same as that which precedes it, punishment will increase the probability of the latter (Logan, 1951; Muenzinger and Powloski, 1951). If the responses preceding and following punishment are different, many experiments show that punishment decreases the probability of the response prior to punishing stimuli. There is no one-to-one correspondence between nonreinforcement on the one hand and punishment on the other, if we take the definitions stated above. The best solution seems to be that of accepting the reinforcement-nonreinforcement dichotomy, and classifying punishing stimuli one way or the other in terms of effects in specific situations. The complex relations between reinforcement and punishment flow from their definitions on two separate criteria.

The results which show that punishment may increase the probability of response raise problems for any theory, including Hull's, which identifies reinforcement in terms of an increase in response probability. A theoretical position which seems to handle these results and which has few postulates can be found. This position states that only two consequences affect reaction tendency: reinforcement and nonreinforcement. Reinforcement acts to increase, and nonreinforcement to decrease, the tendency to repeat a response to a stimulus complex. Punishment would have no direct effect on the punished response tendency but would act indirectly on behavior via the responses which it evokes and which are reinforced by its termination.

According to this description, termination of punishment is reinforcing. Therefore, any response which immediately precedes this reinforcement will obtain an increased reaction tendency. Many experiments show that a response which occurs regularly to some stimulus embedded in a series of stimuli tends to become anticipatory and to occur to stimuli earlier in the series. This law, which should be deducible from a theory like Hull's, implies that responses evoked by punishment prior to its termination later will occur before the punishment.

The effect of punishment upon a preceding response therefore depends upon the nature of the responses evoked in turn by punishment. If these punishment-produced responses are incompatible with the punished responses, then the former will become anticipatory and will reduce or eliminate the occurrence of punished responses through competition. But if the punishment evokes responses which are identical or compatible with the punished responses, then the former will become anticipatory and will increase the likelihood of the punished responses. Since the effect of punishment upon subsequent behavior depends upon the responses evoked by the punishment, the theorist must know what those responses are before he can venture a prediction.

This requirement even complicates matters somewhat in the laboratory, where the psychologist uses painful stimuli like electric shock as punishers. These complications arise from two sources: 1. the response to the shock may depend partly upon the response preceding the shock, and 2. the response to the shock may change with experience. The first case occurs (F. Sheffield, 1948) where shock evokes running in an animal which is standing still but evokes cessation of activity if the animal is running. The second case appears (Muenzinger and Powloski, 1951) where shock initially evokes withdrawal from a charged grid but evokes rapid forward movement after a few trials.

In dealing with human social behavior these two problems are further accentuated. Many punishments imposed upon an individual by his fellows are not physically painful but rather involve learned fears. The effectiveness of these secondary punishments (e.g. social disapproval) therefore will depend upon the past history of the individual. The identification of such stimuli involves the same difficulties as those met in dealing with secondary reinforcers, once we recognize how markedly both types depend on learning.

So far we have not considered the quantitative aspects of reinforcement and their effects on behavior. We have treated reinforcement and nonreinforcement in an all-or-none fashion. But a reinforcing stimulus may vary in its quantitative properties, and these variations affect behavior. Despite the long history of the law of effect, many quantitative relations basic to its operation have not been studied empirically. Nonetheless we find enough data to present a general framework for the analysis of those relations. This analysis will complete the first part of our discussion of reinforcement.

A reinforcing stimulus has a number of measurable aspects such as magnitude, time of occurrence after a response, and sheer occurrence or nonoccurrence after each of a sequence of responses. Also, as we pointed out in Chapter 3, a response has several measurable dimensions. Now we will define conditions of reinforcement as the relationships in a specific situation between *each* aspect of a reinforcing stimulus and *each* dimension of a response. These relationships are determined by an experimenter in the laboratory; in nonlaboratory situations they describe environmental constraints placed on a subject's behavior. These functions may be of any single-valued form; different situations will present different conditions of reinforcement, each of which tells how a given aspect of reinforcement changes as a certain response dimension varies.[5] By way of illustration let us describe a possible laboratory situation.

5. There are certain limitations imposed by the necessity for the conditions of reinforcement to be internally consistent. For example, magnitude and de-

In a certain experiment response amplitude may be related to magnitude of reinforcement by some monotonic increasing function; i.e. as amplitude is increased, a greater reward is offered. Simultaneously, amplitude may bear a horizontal relationship to delay of reinforcement: the delay is some constant value regardless of response amplitude. Further, latency of response may be related directly to delay of reinforcement, so that shorter latencies provide shorter delays. Under such a partial set of conditions of reinforcement the subject can increase magnitude and reduce delay of reinforcement by faster and larger responses. The degree of such improvement, of course, depends upon the slopes of the functions described above.

The number of possible conditions are too numerous to itemize here but the examples given suggest the implications of the concept of conditions of reinforcement. This concept complements Hull's identification of behaviors differing along some dimension as different micromolar responses. The organism may be viewed as choosing values for various dimensions of his behavior, and the conditions of reinforcement describe what he gets for any particular selection. This view suggests further studies on what response a subject chooses under a variety of conditions of reinforcement. The findings may then fit a quantitative description positing such a notion as disutility as a specified function of the response dimensions, and utility as a specified function of the aspects of reinforcement. This type of analysis is traditional among economists and has proved valuable in describing economic behavior. The present analysis differs from economic theory in recognizing the several dimensions of the response and the various aspects of the reinforcement, whereas economists have generally concentrated upon the magnitude of reinforcement and the amplitude or rate of the response.

The description of conditions of reinforcement given above is incomplete, since complete analyses of the possible dimen-

---

lay of reinforcement are independent except at zero magnitude, where delay must be infinity; any time a zero magnitude is prescribed the delay is automatically determined. A complete analysis of the restrictions is not necessary for the purpose here at hand.

sions of the response and aspects of reinforcement were not provided. A catalogue of response dimensions depends on what system is used for defining responses as well as on other factors, a point discussed in Chapter 3. We shall now mention some of the aspects of reinforcement which appear to be important determinants of behavior.

"Magnitude" of reinforcement refers to the amount of the goal object; behavior may vary with this magnitude and may change with any shifts in magnitude (Zeaman, 1949). The "delay" of reinforcement is the time elapsing between the termination of the response and the receipt of the reinforcement; behavior also varies with this delay and changes with any shift in the delay (Logan, 1952). We may expand the time aspects of reinforcement by defining the "latency" of reinforcement as the time between the initiation of the response and the receipt of the reinforcement; and the "interval" of reinforcement may be defined as the time between presentation of a conditioned stimulus and the receipt of the reinforcement. To our knowledge, neither of these latter two aspects has been studied empirically; they are suggested as systematic possibilities.

Other aspects of reinforcement have been studied, including "quality" of reinforcement; subjects prefer one or the other of two goal objects of equal weight (F. Sheffield and Roby, 1950). Another aspect is the "form" of the reward; several pieces of food produce stronger behavior than a single piece of the same total weight (Wolfe and Kaplon, 1941). Finally, there is the "pattern" of reinforcement: the probability that reward will follow a particular occurrence of the response, and the pattern of reinforcements generated by interspersed nonreinforcement. We shall discuss this condition below.

Each of these aspects of reinforcement—and perhaps others—is related to each dimension of the response. The conditions of reinforcement depict what may be called the "terms" confronting the organism: the range of response dimensions available to him and the levels of the reinforcement aspects contingent upon any particular selection.

When we come to the pattern or schedule of reinforcement,

we meet the central problem in tracing the effects of previous reinforcements on behavior. This problem concerns the effects of a temporal sequence of reinforcements and nonreinforcements on one or more dimensions of a response. Hull's formulation of habit strength as a function of number of reinforcements assumed at first that reinforcement occurs at every opportunity; he assumed that during learning a reinforcement is never followed by a nonreinforcement. Likewise, his formulation of conditioned inhibition as a function of nonreinforced trials made a similar assumption regarding the pattern of nonreinforcement. These two assumptions of a regular schedule of reinforcement or nonreinforcement respectively cover restricted cases, and Hull's formulation faces difficulties which we shall discuss shortly.

Obviously an organism may be reinforced on some occasions and not on others according to a pattern imposed by the investigator. Experimental psychologists have studied many cases of partial reinforcement. (See Skinner, 1938, and F. Sheffield, 1948, among others.) Conditions in human society practically guarantee that partial reinforcement prevails for many kinds of social behavior. It may affect different dimensions of a response in quite diverse ways. Rate of response and resistance to extinction generally are enhanced by partial, as against regular, reinforcement. But amplitude or probability within a group of subjects may be affected primarily by the number of reinforcements and nonreinforcements within widely varying patterns. Certainly, the empirical laws of partial reinforcement are relevant to many human situations where some dimensions of behavior are maintained over long periods of time, although others may change. As with many other conditions of reinforcement, we do not have a complete set of such laws.

A series of regular reinforcements followed by a series of regular nonreinforcements is a special pattern of reinforcement. This particular pattern, however, has been studied very frequently; during reinforcement a habit is built up and during nonreinforcement it declines. The extinction or disappearance of a habit under nonreinforcement provides one model for the phenomena of forgetting, which have received wide attention in psychology and psychiatry. Before taking up some theoretical implications of patterns of reinforcement we shall briefly discuss forgetting, in order to emphasize the fact that pattern of reinforcement is probably not the sole determinant of the loss of a habit.

From the point of view of reinforcement theory, we assume initially that forgetting is not a passive process, due solely to the lapse of time since learning. Considerable evidence supports the view that forgetting depends on interference between new and old responses (Woodworth, 1938, pp. 257–76; Hovland, in Stevens, 1950; McGeoch, 1942); the theory that forgetting is a passive process seems unnecessary. But behavior patterns may be lost through any of three possible processes.

One process is the development of new responses which are incompatible with older ones, even though the latter are still reinforced. The new responses become strong enough to prevent performance of the older ones. A given response thus disappears when another, incompatible with it, has been attached to the cue for the first. This process is held to be a paradigm for repression (Dollard and Miller, 1951) although in most cases of repression a large number of conflicting response tendencies may be involved (Freud, 1938).

The second process through which behavior patterns are lost involves a decrease in the probability of a learned response as a result of repetition with lack of reinforcement. In this case apparently nothing new is learned; the organism may return to other responses which it made before the extinguished habit was originally established. The conditioning of any new response to a cue involves the extinction of other responses already attached to that cue.

Finally, the third process by which the probability of a response can be decreased should be mentioned even though the decrease is merely temporary. This process has been called "fatigue" by Sherrington (1947, pp. 215–24), who found that repeated evocation of a reflex at a sufficiently high rate decreased the amplitude or rate of response. If the subject was not stimulated for a short period afterwards, the reflex recovered from fatigue and returned to its usual status.

This process, and several others allied to it, may be involved in many changes of behavior.

Hull's concept of reactive inhibition is similar to the idea of fatigue (1951, pp. 73–86). Objectively, we say fatigue has occurred when a response declines in strength merely because of frequent elicitation. Responses also may decline in strength because of extinction, and it is possible but not always easy to separate the effects of extinction from those of fatigue. This separation can be made, however, when we deal with unconditioned responses, since the response strength at the beginning of separate experimental sessions on different days is the same. Fatigue of an unconditioned response is a function of many factors, and the general assumption that fatigue is a monotonic increasing function of the number of stimulus presentations is not necessarily true either (Lloyd, 1949). The stimulus rate can be adjusted to prevent fatigue and under certain conditions response strength may increase with repeated stimulus applications.

In his theory of behavior, Hull (1951, pp. 73–92) explains extinction of responses through lack of reinforcement as due to accumulation of conditioned inhibition, which is opposite in effect to habit strength; the latter is built up by reinforcement and never decreases. Furthermore, like habit strength, conditioned inhibition can never decrease, making it impossible to predict relearning. Hull also includes in his system the idea of reactive inhibition, which resembles fatigue since it accumulates with repeated responses and dissipates with rest; conditioned inhibition is actually an increasing function of the amount of reactive inhibition present. Hull uses the notion of reactive inhibition to account for spontaneous recovery, the superiority of massed over distributed practice, and the slower acquisition of more effortful responses. The notion of conditioned inhibition will be discussed at length below.

In counterconditioning experiments, a response is conditioned to a cue to which another incompatible response has already been attached. This technique produces disappearance of the response initially attached to the cue, even though that response is never evoked during the counterconditioning. The old response, which now does not occur, does not show spontaneous recovery, but it can be reinstated when the new response is extinguished. As mentioned previously, counterconditioning may provide a paradigm for repression, in which the repressed habit does not spontaneously return merely through lapse of time. The phenomena of repression and hypnosis provide convincing reasons for assuming that forgetting is not due to lapse of time alone. Freud, however, seemed to recognize two types of forgetting: repression and assimilation. The latter type is akin to retroactive inhibition, which also has been treated in part as a counterconditioning phenomenon. Unfortunately, an adequate account of the various modes of forgetting is not yet available, and further work must be done on this problem.

We now return to the implications of phenomena dependent on patterns of reinforcement for Hull's theory. Actually these same implications hold for many theories which describe learning as the net effect of two opposed processes, one positive and the other inhibitory. We will consider only the pattern of reinforcement where there are alternating blocks of regular reinforcements and nonreinforcements.

We have previously discussed two general behavioral laws: 1. if a reinforcing state of affairs closely follows the occurrence of a response, the probability of repetition of that response to the stimulus complex present is increased; and 2. the failure of a reinforcing state of affairs (nonreinforcement) is followed by a reduced response probability. We now consider a temporal extension of these two laws: 3. if a reinforcing state of affairs is reinstated after a phase of nonreinforcement, response probability is again increased. It is generally reported that this relearning proceeds more rapidly than original learning.

An adequate theory of behavior must explain the phenomenon of relearning and this requirement raises a number of problems.[6] The manner in which any system handles relearn-

6. A theorist can choose initially to work only with original learning data; any contemporary theory is applicable to a specifically demarcated class of events. Hull's original system was so restricted. It is the writers' opinion, however, that even early postulates should offer at least qualitative description of all the known general laws in the relevant area.

ing is partially dependent upon its treatment of original learning and extinction; within the formulations of stimulus-response theory the role of nonreinforcement is the most critical determinant, because original learning is described as the acquisition of a hypothetical bond or connection between stimulus and response (which we may call a habit). Relearning phenomena require that the postulated effects of nonreinforcement be counteracted.

There are in general two alternative assumptions concerning the effects of nonreinforcement: a reduction in the originally learned habit, or the accumulation of a second habit (typically called inhibition) which subtracts from the first. If a theorist selects the first position, then the relearning phenomenon forces him to admit a subsequent increase in the habit when reinforcement is reintroduced. Theories of the second type must permit a subsequent reduction in inhibition upon reintroduction of reinforcement or postulate a third habit increased by the second phase of reinforcement. Since this latter procedure involves an infinite progression of acquisition and extinction habits, we shall tentatively reject it as impracticable.

If a theorist holds that nonreinforcement reduces the learned habit, relearning poses the difficulty that the rate of increase in this habit during relearning is faster than during original learning. For example, a single reinforcement during original learning may increase the probability of a response from .25 to .40, whereas after complete learning and subsequent extinction to the .25 probability level, a single reinforcement generally will increase response probability to above the .40 level. Accordingly, the increment per reinforcement in the postulated habit cannot be a simple function of the existing level of this habit but must also be related to the number of preceding reinforcement-nonreinforcement phases.

This complexity is not avoided but only postponed by a theory which holds that nonreinforcement produces inhibition and that subsequent reinforcement can reduce this inhibition. One might assume that inhibition is dissipated by reinforcement faster than the original habit is formed, thereby directly accounting for faster relearning. However, a second relearning after a second extinction may proceed even more rapidly than the first relearning, and the theorist must therefore relate rate of inhibition dissipation to the number of preceding nonreinforcement phases. Accordingly, neither position on nonreinforcement presents much hope for parsimony.

These arguments strongly suggest that in each function for habit growth or decay any parameters which determine rate of approach to asymptote must be partially dependent upon the previous history of reinforcement and nonreinforcement. It is an oversimplification, however, to assume that a straight count of such reinforcement-nonreinforcement phases will be a satisfactory independent variable. The work on partial reinforcement clearly shows that the pattern of these phases is also relevant: irregularly interspersing fifty nonreinforcements among fifty reinforcements does not produce the same effect of rapid relearning as an identical number of phases where each phase is carried to asymptotic performance. A great amount of systematic data is therefore required before an intervening-variable theory can be built which adequately handles the relearning phenomena.

While the discussion above has concentrated upon relearning, a parallel set of statements could be made concerning re-extinction, which may progress at a different rate than that of original extinction. It is particularly complex when one recalls that the introduction of reinforcement-nonreinforcement phases in the partial-reinforcement studies appears to produce greater resistance to extinction (slower accumulation of inhibition or decrease in habit). The need for systematic study is again apparent.

We might, at the present time, suggest one further complication. If some rates of growth or decay are made dependent upon the number and pattern of preceding reinforcement-nonreinforcement phases, it may be useful to assume that these rate changes generalize upon learning and extinction of similar habits. Such a position would be suggested by the work of Harlow (1950) on "learning sets."

The primary importance of keeping relearning in mind

when the nonreinforcement postulate is constructed is to avoid the impasse present in Hull's last version of his theory. He held an inhibition theory of extinction but attempted to *deduce* this inhibition as a competing not-responding habit. Because of the permanence he elsewhere ascribed to habits, his system implies that a response once fully learned and fully extinguished can never be relearned. If, however, inhibition is *postulated* rather than deduced, it need not have the properties which for other reasons the theorist may wish to ascribe to habits.

The behavioral effects of patterns of reinforcement thus present phenomena which create several problems for a theory like Hull's. Anticipating these problems may help in a revision of his theory or the development of a new one. Even without a satisfactory theoretical system, however, the empirical laws of partial reinforcement can aid the analysis of some aspects of human behavior. Linguistic behavior, for example, may be maintained somewhat by irregular patterns of reinforcement, and may help maintain other behavior by providing partial reinforcement for the latter. Certain facets of language appear particularly promising for providing links between psychology and other social sciences. In the next chapter we shall explore some of these links.

CHAPTER 5

LANGUAGE

"CERTAINLY there is, as of 1951, a wide recognition among philosophers, linguists, anthropologists, psychologists, and sociologists that the existence of culture rests indispensably upon the development in early man of the faculty for symbolizing, generalizing, and imaginative substitution" (Kroeber and Kluckhohn, 1952, p. 153).

By language we mean a system of conventional vocal signs used by interacting members of human communities, not written representations of such systems. Writing is an interesting and powerful culture complex in its own right and is not devoid of influence on language, but we exclude its consideration here in the interests of simplicity of exposition and because the possibility of an analogous treatment of it should be obvious.

Language is probably the earliest learned of the cultural systems (Hockett, 1950), and, as has been often noted (White, 1940), plays a predominating role in the learning of nonlinguistic culture. For this reason it seems likely that the theoretical gap between infrahuman and human behavior can best be closed by a consideration of the linguistic aspects of culture. It by no means follows from this that analysis of the rest of culture only awaits the application of techniques analogous to those of linguistics, as some investigators seem to suggest (Hall and Trager, 1953). We shall therefore confine ourselves to the consideration of the role of language in human social affairs, taking for granted the results of linguistic analysis. For our purposes it would not seem to make any major difference whether the analysis is made in terms of the theory of Hjelmslev (1943), Jakobson, Fant, and Halle (1952), Harris (1951), or Bloch (1948, 1950), so long as one is chosen and its implications faced. We have found it convenient to use the Trager-Smith (1951) analysis of English, with modifications designed to bring our description into harmony with Bloch's postulates.[1]

Before undertaking a general discussion of the topic we shall consider briefly a special use to which language has been put, namely as a research tool in social science.

Research Uses of Verbal Reports

Social scientists have made wide use of verbal responses in an attempt to predict behavior. The utility of this technique is limited, however, by the fact that "obvious" relations between word and predicted deed are not always borne out. LaPiere demonstrated this twenty years ago when he found that hotel and restaurant managers would usually accommodate a Chinese couple even though more than 90 per cent of them replied negatively to a written question as to whether they would accept Chinese clientele.[2] Since that time much has been learned empirically concerning the kinds of question-answer sequences which are most dependable for predicting particular behavior, but no satisfactory general principles have yet been developed which tell us in advance the relation between such responses and a given kind of behavior.

It is possible that a theory will help in the development of general principles governing the use of verbal or "test" responses. Though the Hullian theory is not adequate to this task it may help clarify several issues confronting polling and attitudinal studies (see Doob, 1947).

Polling techniques are usually designed to predict some specific behavior by eliciting from the subject a verbal report as to which of alternative responses he would be likely to perform in a given situation. In pre-election polls, for example, the potential voter is typically asked: If the election were

1. Including modifications (up to 1954), the chief of which is that all Trager-Smith "junctures" except "plus juncture" are allowable as rates of phonemes comparable to other features of arrangement, but not as phonemes themselves (Bloch, 1953).

2. It is possible that not all the answers were received from the same individuals whose behavior was observed (LaPiere, 1934, 1938).

held today, for whom would you vote? It is assumed that when the election occurs the subject will behave in the manner indicated by his verbal response; i.e. he will vote for the man whose name he states. Often this is justified, but in order to be able to specify the circumstances in which it is it would be useful to know why people sometimes do behave as they say they will. One might assume that there is some equivalence between verbal test responses and the behavior to be predicted. If the test stimuli are sufficiently similar to the stimuli which evoke the predicted behavior, then equivalent responses may be evoked by generalization.

If this is the process by which correspondence comes about, several factors may interfere with it. Stimuli may differ sufficiently in the test and predicted situations so that different reaction potentials are evoked. Testers seeking to secure maximum correspondence might well try to make the stimuli in the two situations as equivalent as possible. A second source of noncorrespondence may be found in changes in response tendency which occur during the period between testing and prediction. An effort has been made to test for rigidity of tendency (Mosteller et al., 1949), presumably in an attempt to select those individuals least likely to be influenced by changes during the interim period. Until we have some idea of the kinds of learning experiences which intervene, however, it will be difficult to deal with this problem systematically. For some kinds of behavior, minimization of the intervening time period might be expected to provide a partial solution for the problem, although the utility of the resultant short-range predictions might well be limited. Still another difficulty is suggested by Hull's concept of behavioral oscillation (see our discussion in Chapter 3).

It should also be noted that the test itself might act as a learning experience and thus become a source of noncorrespondence against which limitation of the interim period could not avail. The effects of test experience could be eliminated by predicting from the test the behavior of untested persons. Like any sampling, this requires that the tested and observed individuals be similar in regard to membership in any sets which significantly affect the behavior in question.

As our discussion in Chapter 7 will suggest, more sets may be important in this connection than such commonly used ones as those defined by age, sex, and social class.

A special reason for dissimilarity between tested and observed subjects occurs when one or both sets are self-selected. The act of joining a sample may indicate characteristics which also affect the behavior predicted. Thus, Kinsey's first sample was criticized as atypical of the universe of adult American males because interviewees who selected themselves might be presumed to have had high anxiety or a need for catharsis in regard to sexual matters (Wallen, 1949). Kinsey has since sought to limit self-selection by obtaining 100 per cent samples of various pre-existing organizations. The reverse of this problem arises when prediction is attempted concerning a universe whose members select themselves. In the prediction of voting, for example, it has been necessary to try, on the basis of polling, to predict not only what people will do at the polls but also who will get there.

Verbal responses have also been used by attitude testers for the prediction of more than one kind of behavior. Testers in this field have sought to establish general attributes of individuals which are labeled "attitudes" or "personality traits." These are presumed to affect a wide variety of behaviors in a way which is seldom rigorously specified in advance. If the relation of attitude scores to diverse behavior could be specified, this method would be far more economical than the polling technique.

Thus far, attitude testers have concentrated on the important problem of reliability. They have been able to demonstrate that the same procedures or variations of procedure can be used to assign individuals consistently to the same class or rank order.[3] Reliability is, however, a necessary but not sufficient condition for validity.[4] We still know very little about the relation between reliably described attitudes and the kinds of behavior which they predict. The utility of

3. For a discussion of two recent techniques, scalogram and latent structure analysis, see Stouffer et al. (1950).

4. For a discussion of this distinction see McNemar (1946), especially pp. 294–8.

attitude-testing techniques as predictive instruments might be greatly enhanced if they were fitted into a theory as independent variables.

It is possible that the techniques for the reliable reporting of attitudes might be applied to the estimation of some of the variables suggested by Hull's theory. If a reliable measure of drive could be secured from verbal responses, for example, the relation of this measure to particular behavior would be indicated by the theory. In this way validity of the measure could be tested. From the viewpoint of the theorist such techniques might have extreme value. For certain types of research this method could constitute the most economical if not the only way of obtaining information on drive, initial hierarchy, and reward anticipation. Once validated by correlation with the prior conditions presumed to give rise to these intervening variables, verbal responses might be confidently used as convenient measures of them. Some attempts along these lines have been made (e.g. Taylor, 1951).

In addition to its use as a device for estimating certain behavioral parameters, language constitutes interesting and important behavior in its own right. We therefore turn to the subject of the development of language in the individual and its influence on his other behavior.

Language Learning

Language seems to be acquired in accordance with the principles of learning which apply to other behavior (Leopold, 1937–49; McCarthy, 1946; Jakobson, 1941). Vocal activity in the form of crying appears to be very high in the hierarchy of responses at birth. During the first months of his life the child makes responses connected with ingestion and respiration which are primary functions of the vocal organs. When the various movements of the lips and tongue are combined with ordinary respiration or with voiced respiration, the child produces noises that sometimes sound like elements of some language. These responses are now subject to the action of reinforcing stimuli from other human beings, ranging from the appearance and increased attentions of the mother following the child's crying to the interest of attentive elders as the child appears to smile or happens to emit a sound or sequence taken to be like that of some language. The stimuli which we summarize as "presence and increased attentiveness" of some older human being already have very great secondary reinforcing properties, since they are often paired with feeding, relief from discomfort, and other desired attentions.

The older members of the speech community tend to reinforce responses of the child's vocal organs more strongly and frequently as these responses approach those necessary for the production of the sounds of the language. So also for the morphemes of the language; if the infant produces a sequence of sounds that is similar to a taboo word of the language, it is not reinforced, but when he first says something that sounds like "mama" (or its equivalent) it is strongly reinforced.

At about this point the child happens to approximate the sounds just spoken to him by someone else. In most cases this is highly gratifying to the other speaker and is reinforced by him. When the child learns that it is not the specific behavior that the adult reinforces, but the replication of this behavior,[5] he has learned to *copy*, or to attempt to copy. This is a great step forward in his language learning. Prior to this, "latent learning" (see Buxton, 1940) and practice effects (see Ward, 1937; Underwood, 1949, pp. 305–6) may have aided in the acquisition and perfection of *vocal* responses, but from this point forward the youthful speaker is in a position to acquire *linguistic* responses (items in a relatively closed system as opposed to relatively random productions) and to employ the great tactical advantage to be gained from the operation of feed-back mechanisms which supply knowledge (see Trowbridge and Cason, 1932; Lindahl, 1945) regarding the extent and direction of his deviations from the linguistic system.

It is probably too early to attempt to state anything about

5. For example, "mama" gets reinforced as a replication of "mama," but not as a replication of "papa," etc.

the order in which particular phonemic and morphemic elements enter the hierarchy and are differentiated or combined in successive approximations to the adult phonemic system. The studies that are phonetically and phonemically accurate are of insufficient generality, and those which have employed larger samples do not inspire confidence in their phonological sophistication. All studies suffer from the overwhelming preponderance of subjects from Indo-European speech communities. The few exceptions are listed in Jakobson (1941) and Leopold (1952).

Language as a Determinant of Behavior

Once the general system of language (though not all the elements) is acquired by about the age of six, the great importance of its role in human behavior may be seen equally in the learning of all subsequent culture, both linguistic and nonlinguistic, and in the difficulty experienced by humans in solving problems where significant linguistic cues are not available ("repressed" or "unconscious").

In the main, elaborate theory construction is probably premature in this area, which needs empirical study of many little known variables. Nevertheless at least some brief indication of the kinds of analytical processes implied by an S-R-type approach to this problem may be of interest. There seems to be some agreement that the great importance of language in human behavior lies in its cue values. Any utterance serves as a series of stimuli both to the speaker himself and to others. There would be an initial presumption that such stimuli can serve the same functions in the learning process as stimuli generally. In what immediately follows we shall note certain of these functions which have received attention in the literature. Subsequently we shall be concerned primarily with the problems facing investigations of linguistic behavior as it is involved in individual behavioral situations such as problem solving. The solution of such problems should contribute also to the knowledge necessary to make predictions regarding groups.

An approach to the influence of language in human learning would suggest that such influence is to be sought in areas to be called as follows: fixing the level of incentive, reinforcement, discrimination, generalization, cybernetic cues, and concept formation and thinking.

Fixing the level of incentive.[6] It is a commonplace assumption in the literature of anthropology and sociology that certain linguistic events can serve to increase or decrease secondary incentive in the listener. (See section on vicarious learning in Chap. 7.) This conclusion is supported by experimental evidence (Hurlock, 1927).

Reinforcement. Certain items of language, having been associated with primary reinforcements many times during their acquisition, come to have fairly stable secondary reinforcement properties (Schmidt, 1941, and Miller and Dollard, 1941, pp. 28–35). Language probably also affects the influence of delay of reinforcement by providing self-stimulation involving secondary reinforcement.

Discrimination. Language is used rather ubiquitously in connection with objects and events in the human's environment. It sometimes contributes to the learning process through mediated discrimination, which occurs when a relatively obscure stimulus is connected to a response which thus produces a relatively distinctive stimulus complex. The obscure stimulus is then said to have acquired cue value (Miller and Dollard, 1941, p. 73).

Generalization. (See the discussion of stimulus equivalence, Chap. 4.) Language is one of the chief factors in mediated generalization in humans. Birge has shown that the association of the same linguistic response with two very different stimuli results in greater generalization of other responses from one stimulus to the other than when they are called by

6. In the light of prior discussion the term "incentive" needs some elaboration. In the Hullian scheme a distinction is made between motivation in the sense of drive, which condition is a function of certain antecedent conditions, and motivation in the sense of incentive motivation (K), which phenomenon depends upon the anticipated magnitude of the goal object. In many situations (especially where goal-directed drives appear to be involved) it is difficult if not impossible to assign a particular factor in the situation exclusively to one or the other of these motivational categories. We use the term "incentive" here to refer to both these properties of an event of reinforcement which affect the behavioral significance of such an event.

different names (Birge, 1941; Miller and Dollard, 1941; Hull, 1939).

Cybernetic cues. There are many data which confirm the hypothesis that knowledge of the extent and direction of nonreinforced responses is of great influence in facilitating learning. The information provided by linguistic cues is a very important source of such knowledge in humans (See Trowbridge and Cason, 1932; Lindahl, 1945; Underwood, 1949, p. 416; McGeoch, 1942, p. 564). A special case of such cues is constituted by the initial stimuli presented to the subject, often in the form of verbal instructions by the investigator, which have been shown to affect the rate of learning and hypothesized to affect the rate of problem solution (see the discussion of "set" in McGeoch, 1942, pp. 277–9).

Concept formation and thinking. Problems of "concept formation" and "thinking" have rightly been judged crucial in attempts to utilize learning theory in the analysis of human behavior by such diverse theorists as Maier (1940), Wertheimer (1945), Miller and Dollard (1941), and Dollard and Miller (1950). These problems involve such characteristically human phenomena as one-trial or no-trial learning. They are concerned, in general, not with the fate of a previously reinforced response but with the discovery and first production of the "correct" response in a new set of stimulus conditions.

In this area there have been utilized such notions as implicit trials, insight (now as explanation, now as description), formation of a good Gestalt, change of the field, and the like. In the following section we will consider one of these notions, namely the implicit trial. The term "implicit trial" is adopted because it is current in the Hullian literature and will probably convey the intended meaning to most readers. In any event a description of the phenomena referred to by this term will be found in what follows.

Implicit Trials

Introduction. The Hullian theory features as one important analytical component the concept of the overt (rewarded or nonrewarded) learning trial. This concept is useful in the analysis of certain kinds of behavior situations because the observation and counting of such trials increases the reliability of predictions about behavior in these situations. With respect to other kinds of behavior situations, however, the overt trial does not seem to be a useful analytical concept, simply because in such situations overt trials do not apparently take place. Learning without apparent overt performance includes, for example, some behavioral phenomena often referred to as imitation, certain kinds of problem-solving behavior, and so on.

From the point of view of the application of Hullian behavior theory to such situations, an important question arises: What, if any, modifications need to be made in the structure of the theory to adapt it to the analysis of such problems? More particularly, is it necessary and/or desirable in the analysis of such situations to postulate the implicit or nonovert trial? Such a trial is, essentially, a kind of subjective and probably symbolic performance; e.g. it involves the manipulation of linguistic or other symbols. The subject presumably associates certain elements of a symbolic system with himself and with various elements of the environment. He manipulates the former (i.e. sequentially arranges them in some way) and, in consequence, manipulates (in effect) the environment, including his own relation to it. Thus, presumably, the trial-and-error learning process may take place in the absence of any overt performance.[7]

There is no doubt that these processes *can* be described in terms of implicit trials. Also, if one is attempting to adapt a Hullian type of theory to the analysis of apparent nonovert performance learning, an initial presumption that performance is a function of implicit trials in at least the same ways that it is a function of overt trials recommends itself on the grounds of preserving a certain symmetry in the analy-

7. From a research point of view it is an awkward characteristic of such "trials" that the performance in question is *directly* observable only by the subject himself, rather than by the investigator also. This circumstance does not, however, constitute a prima facie case against any possible analytical efficacy of such a postulate. The matter of research design in this area is discussed below.

sis of all behavioral situations. Further, certain observations upon performance make the notion of implicit trials at least plausible. Acquisition, for example, is typically more rapid when learning conditions are such as to permit intertrial rehearsal as opposed to massed practice where no such opportunity is present.

The basic question as we see it, however, is not directly that of the adaptation of Hullian-type theory to the analysis of problem-solving behavior. Rather, it is this: What data do we need concerning problem-solving situations in order to predict successfully the behavior which will occur in such situations? [8] The postulation of implicit trials will be helpful to the extent that such a postulate helps to organize thinking about the problem and to direct attention to significant aspects of the situation in such a way as to assist prediction.[9] In what follows we have represented our several (and in some cases widely divergent) views on the matter of the analysis of apparent nonovert performance learning, and have included such concrete research suggestions as seem promising to us.

Possible analytical usefulness. As we have noted, implicit trials have the awkward characteristic that they are directly observable only by the individual performing them. The possibility must not be overlooked, however, that the subject might be able to report the occurrence of such trials, and hence the investigator might gain knowledge of them. In addition, a symbolic trial may be wholly or partially overt; i.e. the verbal symbols may be uttered aloud. Such overt symbolic behavior is itself recordable by an experimenter, but it is nonetheless symbolic in the sense that it does not involve the actual manipulation of the physical environment. Ac-

8. The question may be asked: What, precisely, does one wish to predict about problem-solving behavior? For example, one might attempt to predict all the overt behavior that will be observed while the subject is en route to a solution or no solution or merely whether a solution will be reached. This would seem to be a matter primarily of the interests of a particular investigator. It must be noted, however, that a decision one way or the other may affect the requirements of a theoretical system adequate to the prediction.

9. In other words we need not waste time on the question: Do such trials "really" take place?

cordingly we generate the notions of implicit and explicit symbolic trials.[10]

While prolonged research is a prerequisite to a complete formulation of the notion of symbolic trials, several assumptions may serve as first approximations in order to render the notion occasionally useful. One such assumption might be that, at least for the normal adult human, symbolic trials always occur whenever the symbolic associations are available. Instrumental behavior, then, is always accompanied by symbolic behavior. Therefore, in order to know whether symbolic trials will occur in a situation, we must devise techniques for discovering whether the symbolic associations have been previously formed. Such a technique might conceivably provide the further information as to whether the symbolic associations are, within the frame of reference provided by the individual's symbolic system, appropriate to the external event. This latter knowledge will suggest the effect a symbolic trial would be expected to have.

Further, by assuming that at least the linguistic components of implicit symbolic trials have the same effect as explicit symbolic trials and are performed in a manner and at a rate linearly related to them, a study of the latter may provide a means for partially specifying the nature of the implicit symbolic trials, and may serve as a first step toward counting them.

But let us now ask whether even this type of quasispecification permits us to use the symbolic-trial notion at all. For one thing our earlier comments suggest that if, with respect to simple instrumental learning as well as other kinds, we can construct a task for which our subjects do not have useful symbolic representation, and if we then compare groups only one of which has been given pretraining in just this symbolic behavior, the pretrained group would be expected to be superior as a result of the ability to perform relevant symbolic trials.[11] Indeed, such an expectation parallels a practi-

10. This description will require elaboration at some later date since the task presented a subject may be symbolic itself.

11. This prediction is relevant to a number of studies concerned with acquired distinctiveness of cues and may provide an alternative explanation of some of those findings.

cal use of the concept of symbolic trials made explicit by Dollard and Miller. They believe that a patient in a psychotherapeutic situation suffers partially because of his lack of associated symbols for such events as anger, fear, and the like. The symbolic-trial notion suggests to them that one value of therapy results from providing these labels in order that the appropriate symbolic trials can occur.

More particularly, in that kind of problem-solving situation in which the solution is recognizable by the nature of the problem or the instructions the subject may perform without ever making an overt error, because of his presumed ability to try out the alternatives symbolically. Dollard and Miller have suggested further that when the number of alternatives is large a human may be able symbolically to try out responses backward from the goal, thereby circumscribing many symbolic errors.

The extent to which these effects may be expected again presumably results from the previous symbolic learning of the subject. In some cases, at least, this may go beyond the simple symbolic association learning to include habits of symbolic manipulation. Specifically, the rules of the symbolic system may be of critical importance regarding the effect of a symbolic trial. Consequently knowledge of such rules may be valuable to the investigator. This may be elaborated as follows:

In focusing attention upon the rules or perhaps some other general properties of the symbolic system in which implicit trials may be supposed to be taking place, we give up the notion of counting such trials. This would, of course, preclude the attempt to predict behavior which is importantly a function of the *number* of trials, rather than just the probable fact of some such trials. However, it seems plausible to us that this is a relatively unimportant behavioral category, since implicit trials may be an important determinant of behavior primarily for reasons other than those accounting for the number of them that take place in any particular behavioral situation. This would seem especially to be the case with respect to behavioral situations which may be categorized as constituting problem choices. In this situation the individual, when confronted with a stimulus, is conscious of having to choose either the route to the goal or goals, or one of two alternative goals, and so on.[12] The simplest kind of prediction regarding behavior in such a case would seem to be related directly to the outcome of the situation; that is, we might try to calculate the probability that the (unobserved) implicit-trial sequence will be terminated by one or another particular behavior pattern.

How can we go about this? We can sketch out only a preliminary and tentative approach in answer to this question. At the outset it seems clear that we must be able to infer what problem confronts the individual where this has not been set by the investigator. This might be done on the basis of the individual's linguistic response to interrogation, or on the basis of inference from his observable instrumental behavior. For example, we might observe him with a stick in his hand jumping up and down in an apparent attempt to place one end of the stick in the vicinity of an apple suspended from a tree limb overhead. Given some knowledge or inference regarding the nature of the problem situation, the probability that a particular response will terminate the behavior in question depends upon two factors: 1. the language system in terms of which the implicit trials are taking place, and 2. the probability (dependent upon the characteristics of the language system) that "manipulation" of the environment in terms of the language will lead to a particular result. Hence we must attempt to infer this datum and to assess the probabilities.

As a simple example let us consider the problem of an individual who has materials for forty feet of fence and wishes to construct a rectangular enclosure of the largest possible area. We know that among his other linguistic skills he is possessed of a knowledge of elementary calculus. We can

12. One might also categorize some behavior situations as "no-problem choices." The organism, when confronted with some stimulus, performs some behavior with no consciousness of a necessity to reason about (or "figure out") the route to the desired goal. It seems likely that for such behaviors the concept of an implicit trial is not of great importance, i.e. is not of great assistance to prediction.

confidently predict that he will construct a square enclosure one hundred square feet in area.

Although this particular example is trivial, the following analysis does help to bring out the essential aspects of this sort of prediction problem and may suggest lines for further development:

1. In this case the language in terms of which the trials were inferred to be taking place was ideally consonant with the environmental problem. It would be hard to find a better language than that of calculus in terms of which to conduct implicit trials where one's objective is to determine a constrained maximum for a piece of construction. This suggests that a language may assist performance not only because it permits any kind of implicit-trial sequence, but because by means of its rules it permits a *particular kind* of implicit-trial sequence peculiarly pertinent to the problem in hand. This in turn suggests that, in attempting such a prediction, we must consider the rules of the language in which the implicit trials are (probably) taking place, in relation to the environmental characteristics of the problem situation. Whether this notion could be usefully extended to the case where the trials are probably occurring in terms of one or another natural language is a question. In our earlier example of a boy jumping with a stick to hit an apple, suppose that a corpus of the language in question reveals its rules to be such as to result in a considerable number of utterances of the sort, e.g. "Father spanks boy for climbing tree." We might predict that the behavioral situation in question would terminate with the individual's obtaining a larger stick and knocking down the apple. But this prediction would seem to be only a pseudo-use of the knowledge about the rules of the language to assist prediction. Actually, all we have done is to attempt to determine the culturally approved route to the goal and then predict that in this instance it will be followed. In the case of either mathematical or nonmathematical language the rules of the language are a formal contextual matter, independent of any particular empirical reference of the elements in the linguistic system.

If, however, we are given a situation in which the elements of the linguistic system are assigned empirical reference, the difference seems to be this. With the mathematical language the rules are an important constraint upon the *empirical significance* of any trial sequence in which the elements of the environment are in this way manipulated. When the empirical reference of the elements in the mathematical language is given, the rules insure that only certain trial sequences (viewed as an empirical phenomenon) will occur; furthermore, many mathematically controlled sequences are peculiarly consonant with certain environmental circumstances. When the elements of a nonmathematical language are given empirical reference, the internal (formal) rules of the language do not seem to be such as to be an important constraint upon the empirical significance of trial sequences which take place.

2. Suppose we find a case in which the rules of the language system are not the main factor determining the empirical significance of the trial sequence which occurs. Here the important problem is to discover what determines the direction of the sequence of implicit-trial events, i.e. following one particular linguistic cue (of assigned empirical reference) with another similar cue (of assigned empirical reference), and so on. The answer is, presumably, learning. But just to know that any cue-response sequence employed is undoubtedly learned is not very helpful analytically. We need to know something about the probability of a particular cue-response sequence taking place in a particular situation in order to infer the probability that a particular behavior will result.

Analytical difficulties. In much discussion of the implicit-trial notion (e.g. Hull and his followers) the investigators have identified implicit trials as analogues of linguistic processes. According to them, language is necessary for thinking, and "thinking" can be described in terms of manipulation of linguistic elements. When a subject is asked to describe his "thoughts," according to this position, he can do so fairly accurately because he is giving an overt verbal report of quasilinguistic processes which only he could directly observe.

It is questionable whether the identification of implicit trials as linguistic processes is justifiable at all, even assuming that reports solicited from a subject are highly correlated with internal processes. Subjects will often describe visual or auditory imagery when asked for reports on how they solved a problem (Woodworth, 1938, pp. 783–825). It seems that even when these reports are taken at face value, implicit trials must include far more than mere quasilanguage processes. The role of imagery has not been discussed at all in recent accounts of implicit trials, assuming the latter concept is to be retained at all. In an experiment by May, for example, subjects reported verbal, motor, and visual methods of handling a very simple problem situation, even though all the stimulus material consisted of written words and was therefore ideal for encouraging "internal language processes" (May, 1917).

In any situation where the prediction of human behavior is the objective, there seems at present only one way, even in principle, to ascertain the presence, number, and content of implicit trials: through a verbal report given by the subject.

Now, human beings who are solving problems do not customarily give voice to their inmost thoughts at every stage of the process. In the experimental situation, if such reports are wanted the subject must be asked for them, and it has not as yet been shown that there is any correlation between his reports and his subsequent behavior, a question that has been discussed earlier. Even if it turns out that there is a correlation the notion of implicit trials adds nothing to the analysis, since our prediction must proceed in terms of the report and the subsequent behavior; anything interposed leads only to unnecessary complication. In any event the implicit trial remains, by definition, a postulated unobservable, and thus, from most points of view, of no scientific utility until at least it has the status of an intervening variable in the formulation: i.e. until the construct is *operationally* bound to both ends of the S-R chain. Since the implicit trial does not have the status of an intervening variable, the investigator attempting to utilize this construct is actually just making correlations between the subject's reports and his behavior.[13]

Summary. In summary, then, we find that acceptance of the notion of implicit trials turns on the extent to which the investigator is willing to attribute properties to the model organism. For some investigators it provides a logical bridge from Hullian theory to predictive experiments with humans as subjects in situations where the time element is greatly extended and where one-trial or no-trial learning is commonplace. For others the notion is not a necessary prerequisite to such experiments. The present authors are distributed among both camps. What is more important, however, is that we are substantially agreed upon the methodology of the actual experiments (see below, p. 102), even though not upon the theoretical interpretation of the results. We therefore turn to the consideration of the influence of language in problem-solving situations.

Toward a Theory of Problem Solving[14]

We have considered above some of the concepts that have been used in previous analyses of problem-solving behavior. In what follows we shall examine one possible approach to the subject, namely an attempt to apply a Hullian-derived behavior theory together with linguistic and transitional probability analyses. The propositions listed below are too incomplete and are not sufficiently accurate to constitute more than an elementary approach to this matter. They do, however, have the merit of leading directly to research on

13. The implicit trial may have somewhat the appearance of a response having a definition of type 4, the internal-state variety. It differs sharply from these, however, in that responses of the internal-state type are in most cases some actual behavior of the organism that has the misfortune to be *labeled* in terms of a presumed internal state. The implicit trial is of course not a case of poor labeling; it is, as pointed out, by definition a postulated unobservable.

14. For a treatment of the problem-solving process as relevant to more complex organizational behavior, see Bakke (1953).

what seem to be important variables in many human problem-solving situations.

1. The subjects in such studies are not naive organisms but have a learning history which includes the "correct" movement-type responses leading to reinforcement (solving the problem).

2. The total pattern of the stimuli is unprecedented in the learning history of the subjects (i.e. it is really a "problem").

3. At least some of the stimuli or some other similar stimuli have been previously experienced by the subjects. These we will call "stimuli U."

4. Stimuli U have not been connected with the goal responses of the problem at hand by previous reinforcements.

5. The subjects command a vast system of previously learned responses (language), which through differential learning are characterized by their own transitional probabilities (Carroll et al., 1951, pp. 11, 13ff.; Osgood et al., 1954), each item serving as both response and stimulus evoking the next element.

6. At least one of the stimuli U evokes some previously learned linguistic response.

7. This response serves as a cue to further linguistic responses, each following response acting as cue for the next.

8. These linguistic responses serve also as stimuli to nonlinguistic responses and objects, in accordance with the "conventional sign" character of the subject's natural language.

9. There is a sequence of linguistic responses including within itself a linguistic item which serves as a stimulus to a response (linguistic or nonlinguistic). This is the goal response for the problem at hand. Such a linguistic item we call the "counterpart" of the goal response.

10. This counterpart is sometimes more probable than any competing response to the same stimulus. (When the response occurs, an "insight" or "restructuring of the field" is said to have taken place.)

11. A linguistic response having been evoked, it may—through its own transitional influence on following elements, through generalization with responses similar along either

phonetic or semantic (linguistic and nonlinguistic distributional correlations) continua, through remote associations, or through the atmosphere effect (Wilson, 1948; Sells, 1936)—evoke linguistic responses leading to the counterpart of the goal response.

12. When the linguistic counterpart of a possible goal response occurs, its appropriateness will be considered in the light of the conventional-sign connections between items of the language and nonlinguistic objects and events; i.e. the language is a mechanism for the transfer of previous learning which in most cases can replace trial-and-error behavior, not always, incidentally, making for a "correct" solution (Sells, 1936; Whorf, 1950).

13. If any one of the above propositions is not true for a particular problem there will be no insight,[15] i.e. no solution unless the subject relapses to overt trial-and-error behavior which meets with success.

Prior to the discussion of an empirical test of certain aspects of the above formulation, the following general point should be made. In such an empirical investigation there is apt to be considerable agreement among investigators as to what would constitute an acceptable experimental design. However, this agreement would not preclude the possibility of a considerable disagreement on the matter of what constitutes an acceptable conceptualization of a formulation such as the above. There seem to be two basic positions on this matter. In order to accommodate either position we have deliberately left the term "linguistic response" somewhat ambiguous.

Some investigators would prefer to restrict the conceptualization of this notion to just those responses which have been vocalized by the subject or by some class of subjects of which the subject in question is presumed to be a member. Although these investigators would not maintain that problems are solved only by humans who are gripped by a fever of constant verbalization, they would doubt the potential

15. The fact that insight or reorganization depends on earlier training has found ample experimental support (McGeoch, 1942, p. 528).

fruitfulness of speculation regarding matters they have not directly observed.

Other investigators would extend the conceptualization of linguistic response to include those responses which, at least if our criteria for response definitions are adhered to (see Chap. 3), are reckoned as unmeasurable, undefinable, and uncountable; further, they would in effect attribute these stimulus events to a nonverbalizing problem-solving subject. Such investigators feel that the alternative to such a conceptualization would result in an undue restriction upon the range of important problem-solving phenomena which may be empirically investigated. There seem to be no a priori grounds upon which a choice between these two positions may be made. Our formulation will admit of either, at the reader's discretion. (See our discussion of implicit trials, which dealt with a similar problem.)

Previous studies of problem solving lack comparability because they either consider language influences haphazardly or fail to take them sufficiently into account. The studies of concept formation (Woodworth, 1938; McGeoch, 1942; Underwood, 1949) seem to be characterized by the desire to learn the conditions for the correlation of natural or artificial linguistic responses with stimuli presented to the subject. A series of ingenious experiments by Luchins (1942) demonstrated the effects of presenting stimuli in such a way as to determine some of the initial linguistic responses, and showed clearly the possibility of manipulating antecedent conditions known to relate to linguistic responses in such a manner as to make possible differential prediction, i.e. to test the theorem that the processes of "thought" proceed *as if* they were linguistic responses.

As we have indicated, disagreements regarding theory do not preclude agreement as to the variables which may be tested experimentally. In fact the thirteen propositions just listed suggest a number of variables which may be studied in problem-solving situations. Among these are:

1. The goal response. Special apparatus might necessitate an unprecedented response as the goal response; if so, com-

promise responses or response generalization might be investigated.

2. The number of stimuli U previously connected with goal or near-goal responses. Speed of solution might vary with this number.

3. The transitional probability system of the subject. One set of language probabilities might make for quicker solution than another.

4. The conventional sign nature of natural languages. The work of Osgood and others seems to suggest that meanings can be fruitfully studied by objective means. Individuals differing on tests of semantic differential might show different speeds of solution if an item on which they differed were a stimulus in the problem.

5. Initial verbalization of the subject. Better prediction might be expected given more data from linguistic stimulus-response chains overtly supplied by the subject.

6. The amount of verbalization up to some chosen point in problem solution.

7. The relevance of the subject's responses to problem solution. (See Moore and Anderson, 1954, for a neat evaluation of relevance in one type of problem-solving experiment.)

8. The apparatus used in the problem. The names of the various parts of the experimental environment and the possibility of their having facilitating or interfering effects in the linguistic process must be explicitly stated.

The bare outline of a research design presented below indicates how some of these variables might be investigated. Other plans for similar experiments may, of course, be generated. The present plan is intended to serve only as an illustration of a profitable direction of study.

Various workers have shown that a given linguistic form tends to be evoked as a response more often by some utterances than by others (G. Miller, 1951, p. 176). This suggests the consideration of a problem-solving situation where such a form does not appear as an overt response.

Suppose that subjects are pretested on Kent-Rosanoff word-association tests. From the population of these subjects two groups are selected, depending on their response to the stimulus word "table."[16] Group A is composed of those subjects whose first response was "chair"; Group B are those who did not respond with "chair" at all or who gave it only after many other responses. If the two groups are then individually presented with a problem involving finding an object hidden under a chair in a room containing, along with a number of other objects of about the same size, a chair (but no table), it might be predicted that if the word "table" were spoken to each subject as he entered the room Group A would display faster average solution of the problem than Group B. Such an experiment could be varied along a number of dimensions: selection of groups (those who gave "chair" only as first response as opposed to those who gave it, but further down in the hierarchy); presentation of the stimulus word ("table" for both groups as above, "table" for one and no word for the other, or "table" for one and some other word for the other, perhaps one to which Group B would be expected to respond with a misleading self-stimulus, etc.); subjects' behavior after hearing stimulus word (silently going about problem versus being asked to verbalize versus being asked to respond with the first word, other than the stimulus word, that occurs to the subject).

The experiments suggested above could be supplemented by others in which the nature of the rules of symbolic manipulation is brought more clearly into the research design. In the proposed experiments the effect of a single linguistic response to a single stimulus word is all that is considered. But Howes and Osgood (1954) have shown that responses vary systematically with differing contexts in which the stimulus word occurs. In addition such variables as phonetic similarity, morphemic form-class membership, and syntactic characteristics might be investigated for their relationships to the exigencies of a particular problem. For a real test of the possibility of using the propositions listed above to serve as a bridge between a Hullian-derived learning theory and problem-solving behavior, calculations of the transitional

16. Russell and Jenkins (cf. Osgood et al., 1954) found that among Minnesota college students 844 out of 1000 gave responses showing "chair" as a response to "table."

probabilities of utterances relevant to the problem would have to be made. These calculations would form a considerable task in themselves, as the technical note to this section (below, pp. 104–8) will testify, but in addition they would make problems of experimental control much more difficult since it would be necessary to test subjects for transitional probability comparability (Jenkins, 1954).

The classification of responses in problem solving is a difficult part of any investigation in which the subject can or must respond overtly. This is particularly true where the responses are of a symbolic sort. The most fruitful approach to the problem to date has been that of Omar Khayyam Moore and his associates (Moore and Anderson, 1954) at the Naval Research Laboratory. The chief accomplishments of Moore and his coworkers lie in their experimental task control, through which every overt response can be unambiguously classified as to relevance to the problem, and all relevant responses can be evaluated as to their efficacy in solving the problem. By means of these controls, empirical generalizations can be formulated as to transitional probabilities between responses and response sequences. Although they are not immediately usable on natural language problems, Moore's techniques are nonetheless highly suggestive and point the way to increased rigor without loss of practicability in the investigation of problem solving.

Technical note: a sample transitional probability analysis. The chief difficulty facing the studies proposed above lies in the lack of analyses of the transitional probabilities on the various levels of linguistic analysis; a beginning in this direction, however, is being made (Carroll, 1953). Beyond these calculations, which consider the results for only a few phonemes at a time, there are needed studies which will consider the total population of items from which a choice can be made at each choice point in the utterance.[17] In order to give some idea of the magnitude of this task we present a sample analysis of phoneme choice in the light of both phonemic and tactical[18] considerations. Although the

17. The semantic units of selection may not correspond one to one with the units that describe what occurs (Carroll, 1953).

18. "Tactical" includes both morphological and syntactic considerations, i.e. all the features of arrangement of morphemes in utterances.

utterance to be analyzed can be taught to infrahuman animals, it is only homo sapiens, as Voegelin (1951) has pointed out, who can make any choices *at all* in such an utterance. The infrahuman organism can select the utterance only as a whole or not at all. The speaker of English can make roughly the choices listed below.

The notion of transitional probabilities is an important one in the analysis of verbal behavior. It has reference to the limitations put upon the occurrence of any element X when given some preceding element or sequence Y (which may, of course, be zero). Consider the utterance, *Polly want a cracker?*, which might be rendered phonemically as /2̂pa˘li′wanə ˈkrae. 3̂kər/, where pitch phonemes are numbered from one to four from low to top, and stress phonemes are /ˈ/ primary, /∧/ secondary, /′/ tertiary, and /˘/ weak.[19] In what follows we shall largely ignore pitch and stress in the interests of simplicity of exposition, although of course they are involved with transitional probabilities just as much and in much the same way as vowel and consonant phonemes.

Before the speaker begins to say anything of the utterance *Polly want a cracker?* the phonemes available for his first choice of one are almost all those of English, perhaps excluding only /ž/ (the middle consonant of measure).[20]

Once /p/ is selected as the first phoneme, the possibilities for what is to occur in second position are greatly limited.[21] The

19. Stress phonemes are written above and before the first segmental phoneme of the Stetsonian pulse and are defined as coexistent, although decrescendo, with all phones until the next indication of stress. We owe to Bloch (personal communication) the notion that /′/ is coexistent with the entire sequence /wanə/, i.e. that there is no onset of weak stress before or after /n/. Ergo, two folksy "syllables" are included in one pulse. Pitch phones are spans having as their domain all phones (except of course voiceless ones) until the next indication of some different pitch phoneme.

20. /ŋ/ occurs initially in some dialects, e.g. /2́ŋayˈ3gow^naw/ *C'n I go now?*

21. The notion that the individual phone is the unit of choice is, even on the purely phonological level, a considerable oversimplification. Joos (1948, pp. 107–8, 109ff.) has shown that the articulatory and acoustic characteristics of phones are significantly influenced by at least the immediately preceding and following phones and in some cases by phones beyond those. It follows that the unit of linguistic choice is at least as long as the contribution of any particular phone to the total articulation, or, in terms of Joos's theory, at least as long as the shortest innervation wave (Carroll, 1953). Irvin, Walker, and Osgood (Osgood et al., 1954) describe units of encoding in terms of

next phoneme can only be drawn from the group /y l r w i o u ɔ ə e æ ɨ a/. For example, the speaker might have said:

/y/ Pew supported Martin for senator.
/l/ Please pass the cake.
/r/ Promise you'll come, Betty.
/w/ Pueblo Bonito is in New Mexico, isn't it?
/i/ Peas and potatoes are what I like.
/o/ Polish is a Slavic language.
/u/ Pool your resources, men.
/ɔ/ Paupers are forcing this country into bankruptcy.
/ə/ Putnam began his career in ichthyology.
/e/ Pettiford plays the double bass.
/æ/ Patrick is his middle name.
/ɨ/ Pillow fights are not allowed here.

Any one of the above utterances is a possibility with /ˆ/ and /2/ with the first pulse. Where /y/ and /w/ are taken as second phoneme, only /u/ and /e/ respectively can follow, but in the other cases the possibilities are more numerous. Since our speaker chose /a/ as second (segmental) phoneme, he could have chosen as third member one of the following:

/p/ Papa . . .
/t/ Potter . . .
/k/ Pockmarked . . .
/d/ Pod . . .
/m/ Pompous . . .
/n/ Pontiffs . . .
/f/ Poffenberger . . .
/s/ Possibly . . .
/š/ Posture . . .
/v/ Poverty . . .
/z/ Positive . . .
/h/ Parting . . .
/w/ Pouting . . .
/y/ Pie . . .

"vocalic skill sequences" (probably individual words and trite phrases) which are encoded as units and run themselves "once initiated" and *"vocalic skill components* which we tentatively identify with syllables rather than phonemes."

Since our speaker chose /l/ as third member, his choices for fourth member were limited to the following:

/ɨ/ Policy . . .
/ə/ Pollock . . .

Since our speaker chose /ɨ/, he created a morpheme boundary and thus vastly increased the possibilities for position 5. These are any vowel or consonants except /ŋ/ or /Ž/, since Polly may be followed by *talks, drinks, eats, Whitworth, Jones,* etc., etc. After /w/ is selected as the first phoneme of the second segmental morpheme, however, the choices are again narrowed. They are restricted to the following vowels by virtue of the fact that /ʹ/ began with /w/:

/i/ weaves . . .
/ɨ/ wiggles . . .
/ɔ/ walks . . .
/o/ won't . . .
/u/ wouldn't . . .
/ə/ was . . .
/e/ West . . .
/æ/ wags . . .

Since the speaker chose /a/ instead of any of those above, the possibilities for position 7 are limited to the following:

/š/ wash . . .
/l/ Wallace . . .
/t/ Watrous . . .
/č/ watch . . .
/d/ wadded . . .
/g/ (polli)wog . . .
/w/ wow'd (Polly wow'd 'em when it was her turn to sing) . . .
/y/ wiped . . .
/b/ wobbles . . .

With /n/ chosen for seventh position, the alternatives for the eighth member seem to be only: /t/ *wanted*, and /ə/, the one chosen. At this point again, the alternatives for position 9 are vastly increased since a morpheme boundary occurs after /ə/, i.e. almost any phoneme in the language may occupy position 9 except, as usual /ŋ/ and /Ž/, since depending on whether /ə/

is taken as *to* or as *a*, any "verb" or "noun" in English may follow. When /k/ is selected for position 9, the possibilities for the tenth member are then:

/l/ clean . . .	/ɨ/ kiss . . .
/w/ quilt . . .	/ə/ cut . . .
/y/ cucumber . . .	/a/ cot . . .
/i/ key . . .	/u/ cool . . .
/e/ kettle . . .	/o/ coat . . .
/æ/ cat . . .	/ɔ/ coffee cup . . .

/r/ having been chosen, the possibilities for eleventh member are:

/i/ cream . . .	/u/ crooked . . .
/ɨ/ crimson . . .	/o/ croak . . .
/ə/ cruller . . .	/ɔ/ crawfish . . .
/a/ crock . . .	

With /æ/ as eleventh member, the next may be:

/n/ cranberry . . .	/s/ crass . . .
/b/ crab . . .	/š/ crash . . .
/y/ crag . . .	/f/ Kraft's (candy) . . .
/m/ cram . . .	

Once /k/ is selected as twelfth member, the distribution of pitches and stresses makes it impossible that anything but a vowel come next. Besides /ə/, which is chosen, the only possibility is /ɨ/, in *Polly want to crack 'im?* With /ə/ in thirteenth position, the possibilities are /m/ in *Polly want to crack 'em?* and /r/, which was in fact chosen.

Of course, after *Polly want a* . . . , the probabilities are very greatly in favor of *cracker,* but the fact that other sequences may occur in this position (for example, in an attempt to be witty) makes the analysis more difficult than it might be if language were not, like other cultural phenomena, the result of ever variable momentary reaction potentials.

CHAPTER 6

FREE BEHAVIOR

IN line with certain of our objectives in this book much of our discussion has assumed, implicitly or explicitly, general conceptual categories of S-R psychology, particularly as represented by Hull. The data on which these categories are based have come primarily from controlled experimentation with single subjects, in which attention is usually focused upon one particular class of responses. By contrast most of the behavior which social scientists study differs in two important respects. In such behavior, some variables which are fixed in classical experimentation are partly determined by the subject; we shall call this free behavior. In addition other individuals are often an important component of the environment. Finally, the subject typically can choose among several possibly rewarding performances. In this chapter we shall be concerned with free behavior situations which, we think, require some essential modifications of an approach such as Hull's.

The Free Behavior of a Single Organism

In the typical experimental situation most of the known parameters of learning are controlled by the investigator. For example in a simple bar-pressing (for food) situation, the investigator may control the following (viewed as independent) variables, among others:

1. Total number of trials per unit time and the temporal distribution of these trials.

2. Number of hours of food deprivation prior to any set of trials, assumed to remain constant to a reasonable first approximation throughout any set of trials. (In general, all critical prior experiences of the subject.)

3. Magnitude of the goal object. (Generally, all critical properties of the environment.)

As noted above, with respect to most of the problems confronted by social scientists experimental control of the individual and the environment is not possible. There are, of course, certain statistical control techniques available to the investigator of such problems, by means of which he may attempt to "hold other things constant." Nevertheless this consideration does not obviate certain fundamental distinctions between the two kinds of situations. We shall find it helpful in examining these distinctions to consider the analysis of one experimental example of a simple free behavior situation.

Suppose a bar-pressing experiment to be designed as follows: The subject lives continuously in the problem box. He presses a bar for food, and this is his only source of food. This free experimental situation is analogous to the simplest of free human behavior situations: say a castaway who divides his time between leisure and the acquisition of the one food item upon which he subsists.

One critical distinction between the free situation and the usual experimental situation is this one. In the usual experimental situation a theoretical format featuring one dependent variable as some function of a number of independent variables is often conceptually appropriate. With respect to the free behavior situation, however, any such formulation seems fundamentally inappropriate. This is because a number of the aspects of the situation that are indeed independent variables in controlled experimentation must be viewed in the free situation as mutually interdependent and simultaneously determined by the behavior of the organism itself. For example, in our free experimental situation as in many free behavior situations, the subject's own behavior (rather than that of the investigator) determines the total number (per unit time) and time distribution of performance opportunities whether rewarded or not. Hence, depending upon the progress of learning, the subject partially determines the number of rewarded performances per unit time. As a result the subject also partially determines the number of hours of food deprivation at any time. We will further elaborate this point following presentation of some other necessary concepts.

In the analysis of the free bar-pressing situation the first question to be answered is: What shall be utilized as a response dimension or measure? The usual possibilities are latency, amplitude, frequency, and resistance to extinction. Of these measures, frequency would seem to be the most appropriate.

In this connection some general discussion of the problem of response measures in free behavior situations will be helpful. In S-R psychology generally, and in the Hullian scheme in particular, a good bit of emphasis is put upon a unit of the subject's experience commonly termed the "trial." A trial is said to begin when the subject is introduced into the stimulus situation and to end when he is removed from it. Thus the number and time sequence of opportunities to perform are controlled by the investigator. In free behavior situations generally it is not possible to say when a "trial" has begun or ended; that is, the trial as just defined is not a relevant unit of the subject's experience. This means that, however we interpret our response dimensions, we cannot define them in terms of the trial. For example, we cannot use latency in the sense of the interval between introduction to the stimulus situation and completed performance; nor could we use frequency in the sense of the ratio reinforced to total trials. In free behavior situations we can, generally speaking, substitute the concept of the performance for that of the trial and define our response measures in these terms. One response dimension which we can definitely record in this situation is the number of performances of bar pressing, reinforced or not (n), and we shall adopt the number of performances per unit time (n/t) as a response dimension.[1] (Frequency in this sense and latency in the sense of the average interval between performances are the same dimension.)

1. In the special case in which the bar delivers a food pellet every time it is pressed, the number of performances (n) and the number of reinforced performances (N) are the same. Generally, the investigator can differently arrange the ratio N/n. This matter will be further discussed in connection with the free behavior models to follow.

The response measure n/t requires some discussion. If we attempt to predict the time of occurrence of a particular future performance, this would be analogous to predicting the outcome of a single trial. The Hullian theory suggests that any such prediction would be in the form of a statement of the probability that a performance would occur at a particular time. Unless this predicted probability happened to be one, an observation upon the outcome of a single opportunity to perform would not serve as a test of this theory.[2] If our objective is to test this theory, then we will have to make predictions about the outcome of a number of performances.

We might attempt to predict the value for n/t (i.e. time rate of performance) over some one particular time interval. There will exist, generally speaking, some continuous function n/t(t) (this means the rate of performances as a function of the passage of time) which may be fitted to our observations upon n/t collected over a series of discrete time intervals. We might attempt to predict the precise shape of n/t(t). Or, less ambitiously, we might attempt to predict some of the general properties of this function, e.g. something about its slope and curvature.[3] The more we attempt to predict concerning the behavior in question, the harder will be our task and the greater the demands upon a theory. This consideration, plus the particular interests of the investigator, would determine in any particular instance precisely what would be predicted.

We suggest that the analysis of this free behavior situation may be approached in terms of what is commonly termed "comparative statics." This kind of analysis is based upon the assumption of behavioral equilibrium. Suppose that in the free behavior bar-pressing situation we observe after

2. See our discussion (Chap. 3) of probability of response as a response measure. This is not to say that, generally speaking, probabilistic predictions about the occurrence of single events are of no use. But such predictions are of use primarily in the context of analysis applied for policy (control) purposes.

3. It appears from unpublished work done in F. S. Keller's laboratories that for some time intervals n/t(t) would be generally cyclical in form in an experimental design such as the one under discussion.

some period of time that n/t(t) becomes equal to a constant.[4] Let us adopt the terminological convention that in such an instance the subject is said to be in behavioral equilibrium, i.e. performing at some constant time rate.[5] In comparative statics attention is focused upon shifts in the equilibrium position, supposed to be consequent upon, for example, changes in the values for certain environmental elements. With reference to the free behavior bar-pressing situation, suppose the size of the food pellet obtained on each bar press is increased. This might be expected to alter the equilibrium rate of performance. In comparative-statics analysis our problem is not to predict what will happen during each successive episode of behavior following the change in pellet size—for in any event the organism presumably will again settle down to some equilibrium rate of performance. Our task is simply to predict at least the direction of any shift in the equilibrium position.

The concept of behavioral equilibrium simplifies behavioral analysis in a number of ways, principally, perhaps, by permitting a comparative-statics approach rather than an approach in terms of a fully dynamical model designed to predict the precise behavioral path of the organism through time.[6] Of course a good bit of information is suppressed in

4. The shape of n/t(t) would be expected to vary with the time unit selected. Presumably there is some time unit such that if the environmental circumstances of the behavior are held constant n/t(t) will become constant. We subsequently discuss the matter of whether the Hullian theory would suggest that this is the case.

5. The notion of behavioral equilibrium could be formulated more generally. Suppose a time unit to be selected such that n/t(t) maintained, say, a generally cyclical form, rather than converging to some one value. Now the subject may be said to be in (a moving) behavioral equilibrium as long as the form of n/t(t) stays the same, i.e. as long as an expression could be found to estimate n/t correctly over a number of future successive time periods. We might then attempt predictions about changes in the values for the parameters in such a function. For our purposes, the simpler notion of behavioral equilibrium will do.

6. It must be noted, however, that an investigation of the stability of a particular behavioral equilibrium may involve some analysis of the situation in terms of behavioral dynamics designed to determine whether there do indeed exist the behavioral forces necessary to drive the organism toward its equilibrium position. For an application of a learning-theory type of formulation for such a purpose, see Duesenberry (1949).

focusing attention upon equilibrium positions alone. Nevertheless, if the situation is such that equilibrium time rates of performance do exist, it is often precisely these rates in which we are directly interested rather than the outcome of each and every behavioral episode. For example, consider the individual demand function in economics.[7] Suppose the price of beans to fall. We are not so much interested in whether Mrs. Jones buys more beans on any particular occasion, such as the next time she goes to the store. Rather, we are interested in whether her equilibrium time rate of bean consumption goes up or down.

One particular feature of the equilibrium notion may be mentioned here. We have previously indicated the difficulties for applications of Hull's theory occasioned by the circumstance that in many human behavioral problems the learning of the subject prior to the time of observation and prediction is extensive. We have suggested that, rather than attempting to unravel this learning history in an attempt to infer $_S\bar{E}_R$ values by applying the principles of learning to it, it will be more feasible to develop direct methods for determining these values. Suppose, however, that the subject may be viewed as in behavioral equilibrium at the time of prediction, and our problem that of predicting the direction of shift in this equilibrium position. In this instance the absolute values of the $_S\bar{E}_R$'s need not concern us. Whatever these values, we need determine only the *change* in them consequent upon changes in the values of environmental parameters. (And this we might aspire to do by an analysis of the learning history of the subject subsequent to the parameter shift in question.)

Now let us look at the free behavior situation from the

7. Comparative-statics analysis based upon the concept of equilibrium positions is characteristic of a considerable portion of economic analysis. Since this is so, the possibility of significant integration of economic theory and psychological theory depends in part upon the development of a comparative-statics type of analysis in psychological theory. In this chapter we attempt among other things to show the possible fruitfulness of such a development. Further, we point out certain relationships between analytical models so developed and analogous developments in economic theory. For a discussion of comparative statics, its relation to dynamic analysis, etc., see Samuelson (1947).

point of view of developing several equilibrium models. The problem of explaining the existence of a behavioral equilibrium will be seen to be that of specifying the equilibrium conditions; and these we will need to specify in order to predict the direction of change in equilibrium values.

The notion of a relation between performance level and drive level is central to the analysis of the free behavior situation, and this matter deserves some preliminary discussion. In a very general sense, the concept of drive in the free behavior situation is analogous to the same concept as utilized in the usual analysis of controlled experimental situations. The hunger drive, for example, may be thought of as some function of food deprivation. Beyond this, however, the free behavior situation demands a considerable modification of the treatment usually accorded the drive concept in the analysis of learning situations. There are two consequences of a reinforced performance:

1. The positive effect of a rewarded performance: learning is more complete the greater the number of reinforced performances.
2. The negative effect of a reinforced performance: a reinforcement which reduces drive reduces the tendency to perform.

A considerable part of the difficulty in constructing satisfactory free behavior models involves the matter of achieving a satisfactory synthesis of these positive and negative effects.

Insofar as the influence of drive is involved, the usual learning analysis primarily concerns the first behavioral phenomenon described above, under the two conditions that hours of deprivation are controlled by the investigator and that reinforced performances are held to be neutral with respect to the drive status of the subject. The essence of the free behavior situation is largely that neither of these conditions obtains. Considerable attention must be focused upon the second behavioral phenomenon which relates to the negative effect of reinforced performances.

In the usual analysis we are concerned with values for drive existing at those particular points in time at which reinforcement takes place. In the free behavior situation the values of h (and hence D) at any point in time depends upon the subject's own past behavior within those limits provided by the environmental constraints; that is, h depends upon the time distribution of reinforced performances prior to the point of time in question. However, for an analysis of continuing time rates of performance in the free behavior situation it will be best to think of D as some average of its various levels at particular points in time. Thus we may write the decreasing function D(N/t); i.e. the average level of drive prevailing for the subject will be a decreasing function of the time rate of reinforced performances. Since the investigator will control N/n, we may also write D(n/t), as a decreasing function.

With this much background, we now offer several models for the analysis of the free behavior situation. These models are not completely satisfactory. In exploring various possibilities, however, we shall at least illustrate the general requirements of the comparative-statics type of analysis. Further, we hope to elucidate certain major problems confronting the construction of such models.

Free Behavior Model 1

This model is intended to be in a form which seems most directly allied to the usual Hullian approach. It seems appropriate to adopt the micromolar type of analysis discussed earlier. The dimension of behavior in which we are interested is the time rate of performance (n/t), and *different rates will accordingly be treated as different "micromolar responses."* [8] We need, then, to estimate the effective excitatory tendency (s$\bar{E}$r) for each rate in order to predict the most probable rate of performance.

Since the relevant components of s$\bar{E}$r are habit strength (sHr), incentive motivation (sKr or K), drive (D), and reactive inhibition (Ir), let us inquire as to the relations of these

8. The micromolar approach is discussed in Chap. 3, pp. 45ff., and Chap. 4, pp. 72ff.

constructs to n/t. The positive relationships are shown in Fig. 1. These were arrived at in the following manner:

In any situation, sHr grows to unity at the limit. Since we are here concerned with terminal (equilibrium) n/t under some specified conditions, not with the rate of attainment of this equilibrium, sHr for each different n/t response will have attained unity.[9] The horizontal function in Fig. 1 represents sHr graphically at each n/t.

The K variable is dependent upon magnitude of reinforcement which, in turn, depends upon n/t. In the simplest set of conditions of reinforcement, the ratio N/n is a constant. In this way the amount of food received per unit time clearly is an increasing linear function of the rate of responding, i.e. Wg(n/t). It is postulated that sKr is a growth function of this amount of food, i.e. K(Wg). Accordingly the functions Wg(n/t) and K(Wg) generate the function K(n/t) shown in Fig. 1.

The unique feature, alluded to earlier, of the free behavior situation is seen in the D function. Drive is no longer directly controlled by the experimenter but is partially dependent upon the subject's behavior. Obviously, the greater the amount of food the subject receives per unit time, the lower will his D be maintained. Since D is thus a function of Wg and Wg is a function of n/t, the relationship D(n/t) is derived, as shown in Fig. 1.

The sEr for each micromolar response can be calculated by multiplying sHr, K, and D. Multiplications of the three functions appearing in Fig. 1 yields the sEr curve shown in Fig. 2. From this must be subtracted Ir, which is a function of the amount of work involved in responding. Since higher rates require greater effort, Ir is dependent upon n/t according to some function as shown in Fig. 2.

Fig. 3 then represents the subtraction of Ir from sEr, and accordingly depicts the s$\bar{E}$r value for each n/t. The most probable rate is that with the highest s$\bar{E}$r value. Since the subject is assumed to maximize s$\bar{E}$r, i.e. to maximize

9. This may not hold for extremely high rates, but since they will disappear from the analysis this question need not detain us.

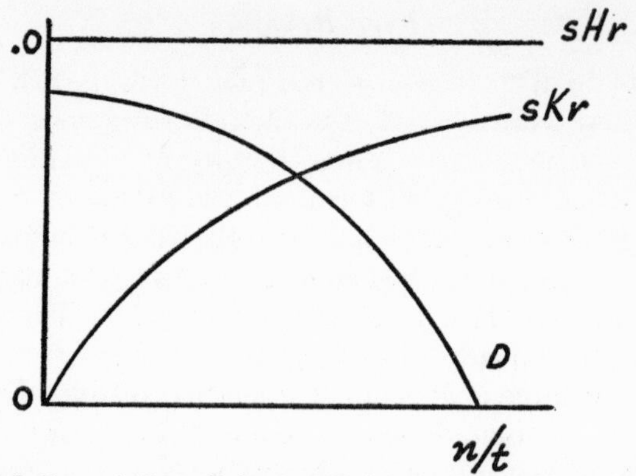

Figure 1. Solution of Free Behavior Model I, showing how habit (sHr), incentive (sKr), and drive (D) are related to response rate (n/t) when each n/t is viewed as a different micromolar response.

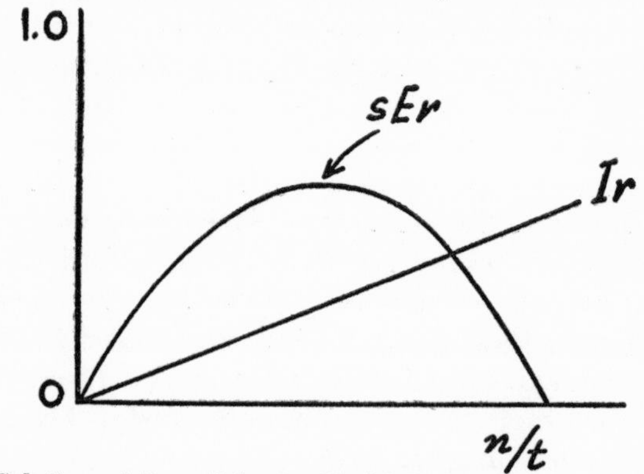

Figure 2. Solution of Free Behavior Model I, showing the excitatory tendency (sEr) and the reactive inhibition (Ir) for each n/t.

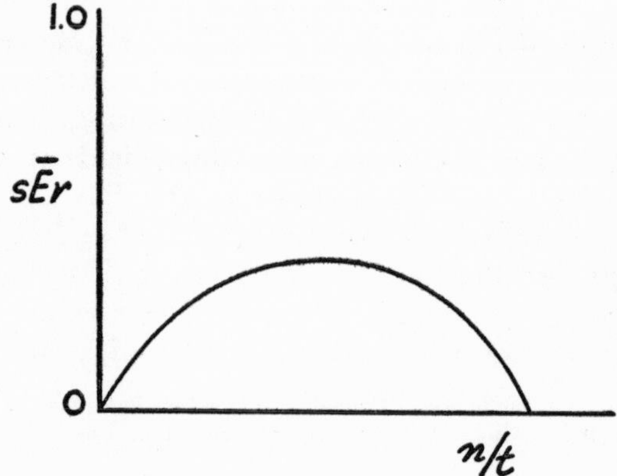

Figure 3. Solution of Free Behavior Model I, showing the effective excitatory tendency for each n/t, from which the most likely n/t can be determined.

(sEr – Ir), we have as our first-order equilibrium condition that $E'(n/t) = I'(n/t)$.[10]

As indicated earlier, we want equilibrium conditions in order to predict at least the direction of shift of the equilibrium position consequent upon a change in some parameter of interest. In the present free behavior bar-pressing situation we might attempt a number of such predictions. Since any one of these will serve to illustrate the techniques involved, we will for expositional simplicity restrict ourselves here and in the next model to one prediction, namely: Suppose two groups of similar subjects perform in free behavior bar-pressing situations of the sort described. The conditions for the two groups are identical except that for one group the magnitude of the goal object per bar press is larger than for the other. The problem is to predict for which group n/t will be the larger in equilibrium.

In attempting this prediction it will be helpful to write out our equilibrium conditions more fully:

$$E'(n/t) = D(n/t) \times K'(n/t) + K(n/t) \times D'(n/t) = I'(n/t).^{11}$$

We neglect H since it will have the same value for all rates of performance, and at the outset let us neglect the problem of alteration in the slopes of the D and K functions. We will mention this matter later. Now, according to the postulates of this model, an increase in the magnitude of the goal object will increase K(n/t) but will decrease D(n/t), and hence unless we have enough information to predict the net effect we cannot predict the effect of a change in the weight of the goal object per bar press upon the equilibrium rate of n/t.

Before passing on to Model 2 we shall discuss certain as-

10. Where X(Y) denotes X as some function of Y, let X′(Y) denote the first derivative of that function. We shall drop the subscripts from sEr, etc., since this will simplify exposition without causing any confusion of meaning.

We should also note that oscillation (sOr) implies that maximum $s\dot{E}r$ will vary from moment to moment; n/t would therefore presumably vary about the most likely equilibrium level.

11. For simplicity, this expression is not written out fully. Let Wg mean rate of acquisition of the goal object. Terms such as K′(n/t) expand to $K'(Wg) \times Wg'(n/t)$, etc. This matter will be discussed later.

pects of Model 1, mainly the matter of incentive motivation, K. In Model 1 the micromolar approach involved treating different n/t's as "different behaviors," and hence the value for K as dependent upon the rate of acquisition of reinforcement associated with varying rates of performance. Thus K, rather than assuming a given value once the weight of the goal object per bar press was given, varied with the subject's own rate of performance. Treated in this way, K becomes essentially an income effect,[12] analogous to certain aspects of the older utility analysis in economics. (Indeed, some readers may have perceived that this seemingly most direct extension of the Hullian analysis to the free behavior situation results in an analytical format closely analogous to the older utility analysis of the individual supply curve of labor. We shall allude further to this matter in what follows.) Incentive motivation is subject to a widely different interpretation in the experimental contexts in which Hullian analysis has usually been applied. In the usual context, which does not involve defining different rates of behavior as different behaviors, K does not vary with the subject's own performance rate. Once the magnitude of the goal object per bar press is set, so is K, and K cannot change as it does in Model 1, independently of a change in the ratio of reward to units of effort in performing the rewarded behavior. Thus, in the usual situation, a change in K can be interpreted as a psychological wage-rate effect, i.e. as having *psychological* importance as a change in the terms of trade rather than as a change in total income received. In Model 1 (as was characteristic of the older utility analysis) the wage-rate effect is viewed strictly as an environmental parameter, not at all as a psychological one. To illustrate this let us return to our previous problem, which came down to a prediction of change in $E'(n/t)$ consequent upon a change in the weight of the goal object per bar press. Consider one term in the expanded version of this expression, e.g. $K'(n/t)$. What will be said

12. The income effect concerns the importance of value received per unit time independently of the work involved, whereas the wage effect concerns the importance of value received per unit work independently of the time involved.

about this term in illustration of our point will likewise apply to D′(n/t). As before, let Wg stand for the rate of acquisition of the goal object. Now, $K'(n/t) = K'(Wg) \times Wg'(n/t)$. The value for the second expression on the right-hand side is the wage rate, treated strictly as an environmental parameter. Of course, a change in magnitude of goal object per bar press alters K′(n/t), but it does so via this environmental parameter, while the psychological parameter in this situation, namely K′(Wg), remains unaltered.

Whether or not a general behavior theory needs a wage-rate effect as a psychological parameter of the subject cannot be settled at this time. But a possible redundancy may be involved in defining (as in the micromolar approach) different behaviors in such a way as to make K an income effect, and then maintaining both this effect and a drive effect in the analysis. In the free behavior bar-pressing situation higher rates of acquisition of reward (associated with higher n/t) mean also lower prevailing rates of hunger drive (associated with higher n/t). These two phenomena might be viewed simply as the two sides of the same coin, rather than as independent data in the explanation of the behavior in question. Thus we might establish equilibrium n/t for the subject with the relation I(n/t) and *either* K(n/t) *or* D(n/t).

From the point of view of recognizing possible relations among the various behavior sciences, it is of interest to note the following: If the view suggested above on the redundancy of including both D(n/t) and K(n/t) in the analysis were adopted, and the former dropped from the analysis, then Model 1 would become very closely analogous to the older utility analysis of the individual supply curve of labor. That analysis postulated that utility was an increasing, negatively accelerated function of income level. Given a wage rate, a function was set up completely analogous to Model 1's K(n/t). It was further postulated that disutility (from work) was an increasing positively accelerated function of amount of work. Hence there was a function analogous to Model 1's I(n/t). It was then postulated that the subject would work, in equilibrium, at that rate which would maximize net utility, i.e. utility minus disutility. This is analogous to Model 1's maximization of $s\bar{E}r$. Beyond the interest inherent in simple recognition of this relation between the two formulations, there is another reason for mentioning this matter. We earlier pointed out that Model 1 would not deliver a prediction about the effect upon equilibrium n/t resulting from a change in the magnitude of reinforcement per bar press because K(n/t) and D(n/t) moved in opposite directions given a change in the magnitude of goal object per bar press. The older utility analysis did not include analogues to both D and K, but only to the latter. Even so, the older utility analysis could not make the prediction in question, and this would suggest that Model 1 would experience the same difficulty even without the opposing effect of D and K. That this is indeed the case is easily seen. Suppose D(n/t) is dropped from Model 1 but K(n/t) is retained. Since H remains a constant, our simpler equilibrium condition becomes: $K'(Wg) \times Wg'(n/t) = I'(n/t)$. Now suppose the weight of the goal object per bar press is increased, e.g. 10 per cent, and the subject continues in the first instance at the same n/t.[13] This means I′(n/t) stays the same. Our problem now concerns $K'(Wg) \times Wg'(n/t)$. If this expression stays the same, the subject will continue at the same n/t. If it increases, the subject will increase n/t and will decrease n/t if it decreases. We know that a 10 per cent increase in the weight of the goal object will increase Wg′(n/t) 10 per cent. Since K(Wg) is postulated to be an increasing negatively accelerated function, and since, given the same initial n/t, an increase in the weight of the goal object will increase Wg, we know that K′(Wg) has decreased. But how much? We must know whether this decrease is or is not enough to offset the increase in Wg′(n/t). In short, as long as we are utilizing this maximization type of equilibrium condition, even if we free our model of the opposing effects of D(n/t) and K(n/t), retaining only one of these, we still must achieve full specification of K(n/t) before we can make the prediction in question.

13. For a discussion of the utility analysis of the individual supply curve of labor, see Robbins (1930, pp. 123–9), who makes the point we are about to make.

Free Behavior Model 2

Let us now turn to Model 2, which, although not based upon maximization as an equilibrium condition, also confronts certain difficulties over the opposing positive and negative effects of reinforced performances. We have previously developed and explained the relation D(n/t), which will also appear in this model. We make the following assumption: The higher the general behavioral activity level of the subject, the greater the drive (within limits). The portion of this activity which is relevant to the effective drive (i.e. contributes more or less directly to a reduction of the drive) will depend upon the learning status of the subject. But in any event, whether this portion is high or low the general behavioral activity level is assumed to vary as indicated with drive.

As pointed out in our earlier discussion of response definition and measurement, danger inheres in the practice of treating as actual units of behavior theoretical constructs whose presumed empirical counterparts cannot be operationally identified. Hence we wish to emphasize that the construct herein adopted, namely "a unit of seeking or striving behavior (B)," is a theoretical construct. It is not proposed that B's be counted; it is proposed in this model that postulation of them will assist in an adequate conceptualization of the free behavior problem and in the prediction of units of behavior which can be counted, in this case n/t.[14] It is postulated that during any interval of time in which the subject is experiencing hunger drive he will engage in a certain amount of general activity. Some proportion of this will constitute a class of activity which may be thought of as "attempts to perform" those responses which will result in reduction of the drive in question. The term B denotes a unit of

14. There is perhaps no doubt that in an experimental design such as the present one involving an infrahuman subject, B must retain strictly the status of a theoretical construct. In the case of human subjects, however, the concept of B might be given more direct empirical plausibility, inasmuch as such subjects have the power of verbalization. In any event, we are of course primarily interested in developing models suitable for the analysis of human behavior, although upon occasions infrahuman experimental contexts may provide an initial simplicity essential to concept development.

such attempts, and it is postulated that B/t(D) is an increasing function; that is, as drive increases, the amount of the subject's striving will likewise increase. The two relations D(n/t) and B/t(D) suggest the first critical functional relation for Model 2: "D" = "D"(n/t, B/t).[15]

The function "D""D" appears in Fig. 4. The only property of this function considered significant for immediate purposes is its negative slope. In Fig. 4 we measure n/t on the vertical axis and B/t on the horizontal axis. The slope of "D""D" is negative by postulation because the greater n/t (and hence N/t), other things being equal, the lower will be D; and the lower D, the less will be seeking or striving B. This relation represents the negative effect of reinforcement in the free behavior situation.

We have two variables, n/t and B/t. Thus far a psychological property of the subject connected with drive has furnished one source of relation between these. Additional psychological properties of the subject will suggest other such relations, and in particular one which will allow us to take into account the positive effects of reinforced performances. For this purpose we direct attention to n/B, which represents the ratio of bar-pressing performances to units of attempting or striving, and which may be thought of as a skill coefficient. We know that generally speaking, given a constant environment, performance of a given response (variously measured) will, through the learning process, approach some stable level.[16] Because this is a continuing free behavior situation, sufficient N will occur in time for n/B to reach its

15. The notation "D" has been adopted to preserve the general analogue with some role of drive in S-R psychology, at the same time distinguishing this composite relation from any particular Hullian relation. In this first statement of the relation "D," certain shift parameters, introduced subsequently, are presumed constant and have been left out for simplicity. In the above text relations such as D(n/t) should, perhaps, have been stated as (D, n/t) $= k$ to avoid the implication that drive is viewed as a dependent variable whereas in fact it has the status of a simultaneously determined variable. However, the mode adopted has the advantage of suggesting the "intervening" status of so-called "intervening variables" in the analysis of free behavior situations; that is, a construct such as drive has the property that although on the one hand it is viewed as a determinant of behavior, on the other it is determined by behavior.

16. Of course if the environment were constantly changing (a possibility

limit, some constant value. Since n/B = n/t : B/t, we have the second critical relation needed for Model 2:

$$\text{“H”} = \text{“H”}(n/t, B/t).$$[17]

In Fig. 4 the function "H" is represented as O"H," and the slope of this function is equal to n/B. The particular "H" illustrated is one of a class of functions of the form $Y = aX + b$. In the relation shown in Fig. 4, $b = 0$, and we may for the moment ignore the value for a since this will be discussed shortly.

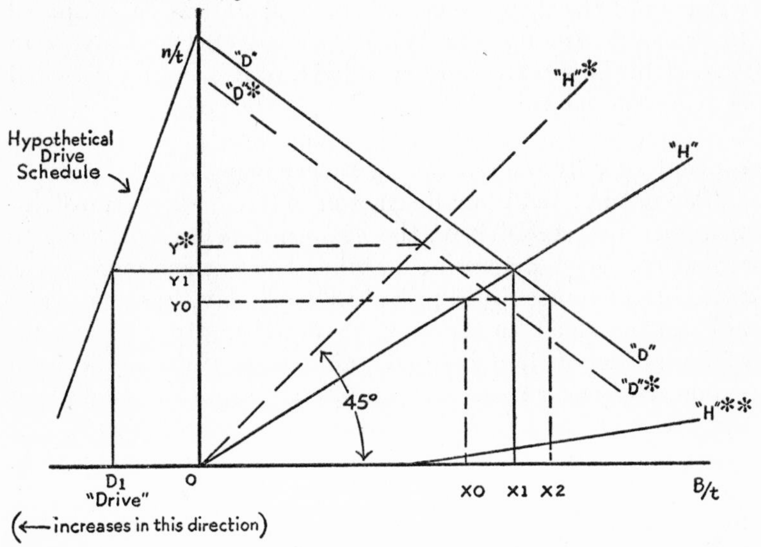

Figure 4. Solution of Free Behavior Model II, showing two sources of relation between response rate (n/t) and "striving behavior" rate (B/t). The "D" function is based upon a drive concept and the "H" function upon a skill concept. The intersection of these two functions yields the equilibrium n/t. (See text for description of the other parts of this figure.)

---

enhanced by the consideration that generally the environment of most organisms contains other organisms as one of its most important components), the subject's behavior might never converge by trial and error to a behavioral equilibrium. This has been suggested as a possible reason why the application of trial-and-error learning theory to the analysis of certain kinds of behavioral situations might not be fruitful (see Alchian, 1950).

17. The terminology "H" is adopted to preserve the general analogue with the associative or learning factor in S-R psychology, but to distinguish the composite relation in question from an H function such as is utilized in Hullian analyses.

We now have our basic formulation, the two simultaneously determined variables n/t and B/t, and two sources of relation between these. Generally speaking the system should be determined at the point where these functions intersect, assuming these relations to be independent and consistent. Before investigating the stability of this equilibrium, however, it will be well to consider the following. In a system of this nature an intervening variable such as drive does not appear explicitly as a variable at all, but rather implicitly as a postulated source of functional relations among certain elements of the theoretical system. This relation is supposed to be due to some property of the subject. Similarly, with respect to the intervening variable H, n/B is not to be viewed as a numerical value for something called H. Rather, n/B is a certain relation between n/t and B/t, again suggested conceptually by some property of the organism.[18]

To continue with our discussion of Model 2, we must investigate the stability of the supposed behavioral equilibrium. We must determine whether the supposition of the existence of nonequilibrium values (due, say, to some external random shock to the system) would imply the presence of forces such as to drive such values toward the equilibrium values. Referring again to Fig. 4, and noting the solid black line "D""D" and O"H" functions, let us take X0 as the value of B/t which is less than the equilibrium value X1. According to the relation O"H" this implies a certain value for n/t, in this case Y0. But, according to the relation "D""D," a value for n/t equal to Y0 implies a drive level such as to motivate the behavior B/t at the level X2, which is greater than X0. Hence a level of B/t such as X0 could not long persist, but rather B/t would increase toward its equilibrium level. The reader may test out a value for B/t greater than the equilibrium level, say X2, to determine that forces are implied to drive it back to the equilibrium value.

18. Thus our use of intervening variables in this case is not to be confused with the sort of conceptualization of them implied by the usual formal treatment, where some relation such as R(h) has in principle broken down into two relations, namely R(D) and D(h). Then, again in principle, actual numerical values are to be ascribed to D and incorporated formally into the theoretical system.

So far Model 2 has not taken explicit account of the factor of incentive motivation (K) which appears as an important element in the usual Hullian formulation. In this model the magnitude of the goal object, upon which K depends, is best viewed as a shift parameter in both the "D""D" and O"H" relations. We can elucidate this point by returning to the prediction utilized in conjuction with Model 1. With two groups of subjects, one of which has a larger magnitude of goal object than the other, can we predict for which group the equilibrium value of n/t will be the greatest? In Hull's formulation a larger magnitude of goal object and hence of K would, other things being equal, be expected to be associated with a higher strength of tendency to perform, on some interpretation of that measure. In Model 2, with O"H" of the general form $Y = aX + b$, the value of the coefficient a (i.e. the slope of O"H") is viewed as dependent upon the magnitude of the goal object. More particularly, a larger magnitude of goal object would be expected to be associated with a greater slope for relations such as O"H", say a slope such as O"H"*. Other things remaining constant, this would be expected to increase n/t. Other things will not remain constant, however. An increase in magnitude of the goal object will also have a negative effect upon the "D""D" relation, shifting it downward and to the left—say to "D"*"D"*. The reason for this is that with greater magnitude of the goal object there will be greater drive reduction associated with any level of performance n/t, hence a smaller value of B/t associated with any level n/t. This effect would, other things being equal, tend to decrease n/t. The net result will depend upon the relative strength of these two effects, and in general we cannot predict the outcome without this knowledge. It is a most awkward characteristic of such free behavior situations that any alteration of magnitude of goal object may set up positive and negative effects in *opposite directions*, precluding prediction without a fully quantified theory. This point was made in a different way in connection with Model 1.

Another aspect of this model remains to be considered. We have thus far left out of account the negative factor of work inhibition. It seems best to handle this factor as another shift parameter in the "D""D" function; i.e. an increase in inhibition (in this situation due, say, to an increase in bar resistance) should be expected to shift "D""D" down and to the left. This means that if the performance of B/t, in addition to reducing drive as a result of the associated level of n/t, also results in the accumulation of inhibition to oppose the performance, then we should expect still smaller values of B/t to be associated with any value of n/t.[19]

Before passing on to Model 3 we shall examine certain additional aspects of Model 2. In connection with models of this nature, it is important to maintain a distinction with respect to intervening constructs such as drive: between drive in the sense of the function D(n/t) and drive level in the sense of a particular point on that function. As the analysis was set up in Model 2, drive nowhere appeared explicitly as a variable but rather was conceptualized as a property of the subject responsible for a critical functional relation between other variables. However, a hypothetical drive function may be explicitly introduced, as was done in Model 1. This may be seen in Fig. 4, where to the left of the vertical axis a hypothetical drive function has been constructed. This indicates that drive is a decreasing function of the time rate of bar-pressing responses. In equilibrium, e.g. at B/t equal to X1 and n/t equal to Y1, the subject's own behavior will establish a certain average level of drive. A variation in the equilibrium rate of performance will change the average level of drive prevailing, but it will not necessarily shift the drive function, and in this latter sense, as a psychological parameter of the subject, drive is held constant throughout the analysis. The converse of the above proposition, namely that a downward

19. Let $X(Y, \tilde{Z})$ mean X as some function of Y and Z, Z held constant. In these terms, our basic relations as thus far described would be: 1. "D" = "D"(n/t, B/t, $\tilde{w}$, $\tilde{I}$), and 2. "H" = "H"(n/t, B/t, $\tilde{w}$). In general, other shift parameters might be added to these relations. Implicitly each contains psychological parameters reflecting postulated properties of the organism, i.e. learning ability and susceptibility to drive. In addition, such environmental parameters as N/n might be incorporated. The utilization of n/t rather than N/t was designed to suggest this latter possibility. In any event the general principles of the analysis remain the same, and Model 2 has been elaborated sufficiently to illustrate these.

shift in the drive function will not necessarily result in a decrease in average drive level in the resulting new equilibrium, may be significant in certain kinds of psychotherapeutic situations.[20]

The major differences between Models 1 and 2 involve the matter of an explicit versus an implicit treatment of intervening variables, the number of behavioral dimensions selected for attention, and the associated difference in the treatment of the factor K. In Model 1 the intervening variables were treated explicitly and were scaled along the vertical axis of the illustrative figure. One behavioral dimension, n/t, was selected for attention. This single dimension of behavior, viewed as directly influenced by D, K, etc., was itself the dimension to be predicted. In Model 2, intervening variables such as D were treated implicitly as sources of the relation between the behavioral dimensions selected for attention, namely n/t, n/B, and B/t. Drive was viewed as motivating a different "behavior" (i.e. B/t) from those performances which reduced it (i.e. n/t), and the K factor was considered responsible for n/B. In consequence the various factors in the analysis, such as D, K, etc., were held to be operating upon different dimensions of behavior, and the performance to be predicted was some function of these.

Returning to further consideration of the K factor in Model 2, we must examine more closely relations such as O"H", of the general form $Y = aX + b$. These relations raise problems not all of which are susceptible to completely satisfactory interpretation, but we may at least point out some of their implications. Thus far no interpretation has been given the term b. There seems no a priori reason to suppose that relations such as O"H" must pass through the origin, i.e. have $b = 0$. It is plausible that during early

20. Certain therapeutic procedures may obtain their effects partly by a downward shift of the drive function, i.e. a reduction in the amount of drive experienced by the subject in consequence of given antecedent conditions. However, reference to Fig. 4 will show that a downward shift of the drive function will also result in a downward shift of a function such as "D""D". The resulting decrease in equilibrium performance rate may result in an actual drive level in the new situation no lower than that obtaining in the original one.

stages of learning positive rates for B/t might exist with zero rates for n/t; as a result b might be viewed as one kind of reciprocal index of habit strength which diminishes as habit strength increases and which reaches a zero value in the limit. Beyond this, a as a function of the magnitude of the goal object is viewed as an asymptotic value, also to be approached in the limit as learning progresses. Thus, in the early stages of learning, the O"H" function might occupy some such position as O"H"** (Fig. 4) and to move during learning to some such position as O"H". Learning is said to be complete under a particular set of conditions once a and b have reached their limiting values. If the positive effects of reinforced performance partially determine the final equilibrium position, then the limiting values of a and b should vary with the conditions of learning and with the kind of behavior involved in the situation. It is clear that b cannot in any event be less than 0, nor a in any event more than 1; i.e. n/B cannot be more than 1. If, when learning is complete, these two values were indeed the limits always reached, Model 2 reduces to a much simpler conceptualization of the free behavior problem. Such a case is illustrated by the forty-five degree relation O"H"* in Fig. 4. In this case, Model 2 delivers a definite prediction as to the effect upon n/t of an increase in the magnitude of the goal object, which, since n/B can no longer be increased, must produce a decrease in n/t by shifting "D""D" downward and to the left. The learning status of the subject was viewed merely as a permissive factor rather than as a basic determinant of long-run time rates of behavior. When $b = 0$ and $a = 1$, we may substitute n/t for B/t in Model 2's hypothetical relation B/t(D). This would then give us the two relations D(n/t) and n/t(D), suggesting that Model 2 breaks down to some relation f(n/t, n/t) $= k$.

As we have emphasized, in the free behavior situation n/t must be viewed as both an input to and an output from the subject. There will be only one value of n/t which, in its role as input, determines just that D level necessary to motivate precisely this same rate of performance n/t. In this simpler conceptualization of the free behavior situation the equilibrium condition is essentially a postulate that the subject will adjust his behavior (n/t) so as to maintain some homeostasis with respect to hunger-drive status.[21] In both Models 1 and 2 it was noted that the factor N/n might be varied by the investigator. However, this factor was held constant. In Model 3 this factor will be introduced as an important integral part of the analysis.

Free Behavior Model 3

This model for free behavior situations utilizes certain environmental constraints exclusively for constructing one function, and bases a second function on other environmental constraints and certain properties of the subject. The model predicts rate of response in a simple bar-pressing situation involving one manipulandum and one kind of reinforcing stimulus. It bases this prediction on three environmental variables: schedules of reinforcement, magnitude of each reinforcement (denoted M), and amount of work necessary for each response (W); M is measured in physical units of size and W in physical units of work. This simple situation may be complicated by introducing discrimination, delay of reinforcement, and "choice" between several manipulanda. In this choice situation, the responses involving different manipulanda may be followed by the same type of reinforcing stimulus, such as food, or with different types. After initial development of Model 3, we will discuss both types of reinforcing situations as well as discrimination and delay of reinforcement.

Fig. 5 is a geometric representation of Model 3. This shows three functions: D, C_r, and C_i; D is determined by M, W, and some properties of the subject; C_r and C_i are determined by schedules of reinforcement. All three functions are plotted in terms of two measurable variables: n/t, or rate of response, and N/t, or rate of reinforcement; N/t indicates the rate at which single reinforcers are delivered, irrespective of their magnitude.

21. Boulding (1950) has suggested that a homeostasis postulate represents the simplest possible theory of the organism.

The function D is analogous to "D""D" in Model 2 and represents the effects of reinforcement on rate of response due to a lowering of motivation. This function has a negative slope, since the faster the subject (denoted O) is reinforced,

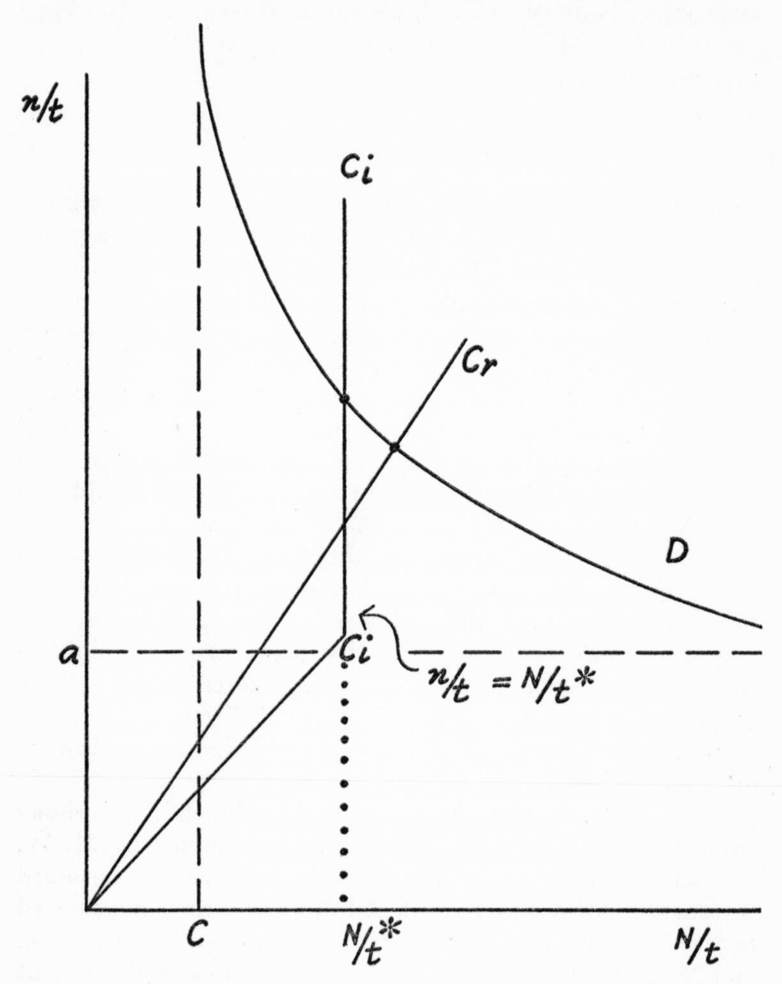

Figure 5. Solution of Free Behavior Model III, showing two sources of relation between response rate (n/t) and reinforcement rate (N/t). The C_r function is based on the reinforcement ratio (the C_i function when an interval schedule is used), and the D function is based upon a drive concept. The intersection of the two functions yields the equilibrium n/t.

the more satiated he becomes and the less likely is he to respond. D presumably approaches an asymptote as N/t increases; this asymptote, labeled a in Fig. 5, shows the rate at which O responds when satiated. This rate may or may not be zero. On the other hand, if O is reinforced too slowly, the total amount of reinforcement becomes insufficient to compensate for the work done. If the reinforcer is food, for example, O could slowly starve at a certain low rate of reinforcement. This minimal reinforcement rate determines the second asymptote c, in Fig. 5. When N/t approaches this value, the equilibrium system will break down and the model cannot be used. Actually the D function in this model could be written with a maximum at some physiologically minimal value of N/t, but this is unnecessary for our purposes. Thus c shows the minimal rate of reinforcement which will keep the subject alive and responding.

We now have two asymptotes for D. By making D negatively accelerated as well as negatively sloped we may write its equation as that of a simple hyperbola. This equation says that response rate falls to its minimum at satiation more and more gradually as N/t increases, which does not seem unreasonable on the basis of various experimental data. Thus the equation for D is:

$$1.\quad (\mathrm{n/t} - a)(\mathrm{N/t} - c) = k,$$

where a, c, and k are constants, with k determining the acceleration of D. Now we must relate these constants to W and M.

As noted above, a shows n/t when the animal is satiated. This parameter presumably would fall as W increases. Thus we would have as the simplest possible situation:

$$2.\quad a = a'/\mathrm{W},$$

where a' is a proportionality factor which would vary from individual to individual. Making a independent of M represents an assumption that n/t at satiation would be the same, no matter how satiation was reached. Experimental evidence can disprove this assumption and show that a depends also on M. Furthermore, the relation between a and W may be nonlinear; we shall assume it linear here, however, as a first approximation.

Now c would decrease as M increases, since with larger unit reinforcements O could be maintained at a lower rate of reinforcement. But if W is increased, c must increase to maintain the animal's total economy. As a first approximation we may write:

$$3.\ c = c'\mathrm{W}/\mathrm{M},$$

where c' is a proportionality factor.

Finally, arguments similar to these generating equation 3 yield a similar equation for k. As work increases, the subject responds at a faster rate to try to balance the input he receives in reinforcement for his output. But as M increases he can drop his output rate and maintain himself. With k' as a proportionality factor, we have:

$$4.\ k = k'\mathrm{W}/\mathrm{M}.$$

Equations 2, 3, and 4 each have their terms in the first degree. This assumption of linearity may hold over a sufficiently wide range of environmental conditions to make the model useful. The assumption can always be changed, of course, but we shall hold to it for the present.

The other two functions, C_r and C_i, are determined directly by schedules of reinforcement. C_r holds for ratio schedules, where the subject is reinforced after a fixed number of responses. This fixed number is expressed by the ratio N/n, which equals 1.00 for regular reinforcement and is less than 1.00 for partial reinforcement. The equation for C_r is therefore:

$$5.\ \mathrm{n}/\mathrm{t} = r(\mathrm{N}/\mathrm{t}),$$

where the parameter r is given by:

$$6.\ r = \mathrm{n}/\mathrm{N}.$$

As the severity of the schedule increases, r increases and the slope of C_r climbs further from 1.00, its limiting value.[22]

22. C_r is an example of what we have referred to in earlier discussion as an "opportunity function." Were N/t interpreted as rate of acquisition of

C_i is a function determined by interval schedules. In an interval schedule the animal is reinforced only after at least a fixed amount of time has elapsed since the last reinforcement. If, for example, O is on a one-minute schedule, at least one minute passes between successive reinforcements. If O responds more slowly than once a minute, however, he automatically puts himself on regular reinforcement, since each response will be reinforced. If he responds faster than once a minute, the first response he makes a minute or more after his last reinforcement will be reinforced itself. The intervening responses have no effect on N/t, the rate of reinforcement. Thus an interval schedule determines a maximal rate of reinforcement, N/t*, allowed by the fixed interval; for n/t greater than N/t*, C_i is a vertical line, since O's behavior does not affect his rate of reinforcement;[23] for n/t equal to or less than N/t*, C_i is a line with a slope of 1.00. We then have for C_i:

$$7.\ n/t = N/t, \text{ where } n/t < N/t^*, \text{ and}$$
$$N/t = N/t^*, \text{ where } n/t > N/t^*.$$

The equations presented above define Model 3 and allow quantification of D. If the model is correct, we hold W and M constant and determine equilibrium values, defined by the intersection of D and C_r, for several values of N/n. The equilibrium values of n/t and N/t should be fitted by a hyperbola of the form given by equation 1. This will be the function D for fixed values of W and M. Then, using the model, we can predict the quantitative effects of shifting W or M. The data from experiments where those variables are shifted and new equilibria established should quickly show whether equations 2, 3, and 4 are incorrect. If some or all of these equations are inadequate, new ones can be set up and tested through similar techniques. The original determi-

---

the goal object, C_r would be strictly analogous to the opportunity function utilized in the so-called "preference system analysis" of the individual supply curve of labor. The reader is reminded that C_r is interpreted as rate of reinforcements, regardless of the magnitude of each.

23. This may not be strictly true when O responds between a rate equal to N/t* and one equal to 2N/t*. For simplicity, we have omitted representation of this fact from Model 3.

nation of D will give the proportionality constants a', c', and k'. All experiments would have to be conducted on the same animal or group of animals. With a group, a', c', *and* k' would be interpreted as estimated population parameters. These might be relatively fixed for different groups of animals of one variety.

We shall now consider the problems raised by discrimination, delay of reinforcement, and choice behavior for Model 3. In a discrimination the subject faces the different schedules of reinforcement at different times. When one schedule is operative, an external stimulus S_1 is present; when the other schedule is operative, S_1 is absent. We denote the latter condition $-S_1$. Usually the schedule in effect during $-S_1$ is complete lack of reinforcement, $N/t = 0.00$. When this happens O responds at a very low rate. Thus when $N/t = 0.00$, the presence of $-S_1$ prevents the animal from receiving reinforcement and drives his rate n/t toward zero.

Now let us suppose that S_1 is present a certain proportion of the time, p, and that $-S_1$ is present the remaining proportion of the time, 1.00–p. We assume that n/t during $-S_1$ is low enough to have little effect in the long run. If $p = 1.00$ there is no discrimination, and equilibrium rates of n/t and N/t can be determined as previously. But if p is less than 1.00 the animal must increase n/t during S_1 to bring its overall rate of reinforcement N/t up to the value which would obtain if $p = 1.00$. If p is 0.50, for example, the subject must respond twice as fast during S_1 as he would if p were 1.00. Thus, in a discrimination, if n/t(1.00) would be the rate of response for $p = 1.00$, and n/t(p) is the rate during S_1, we would have:

$$8.\ n/t(p) = 1/p \times n/t(1.00).$$

Equation 8 is valid as long as the time during which $-S_1$ occurs is not sufficient to put the subject under deprivation. If a single presentation of $-S_1$ lasts long enough, the subject is put back on a deprivation schedule similar to those used in traditional experiments. The precise length of time necessary for $-S_1$ to introduce an effective deprivation schedule would have to be determined experimentally.

Before passing on to choice behavior, we shall comment briefly on the effects of delay of reinforcement. When delay is introduced the animal must wait a certain fixed time after making a response which is "marked" for reinforcement, before reinforcement is actually given. If he responds before that fixed time has passed, the original response is not reinforced and the new one becomes marked. Thus with a two-second delay, when O makes a response which is to be reinforced he must not make another for two seconds. If he does, no reinforcement is given and he must now wait for the reinforcement an additional two seconds without responding. Delay thus forces the animal to adjust n/t to a certain maximal rate when reinforcement is regular. From the point of view of free behavior, the problem is whether that maximal rate is at or above the n/t necessary for equilibrium. If it is, then the model is still valid; if it is not, the subject suffers inanition.

We shall conclude our discussion of Model 3 with a few comments on choice behavior. Two classes of choice situations must be distinguished. In the first, two responses are available and both produce the same reinforcer, such as food; in the second, each response produces a different type of reinforcer. As an example of the second, a response to one bar is reinforced with food and that to another bar is reinforced with water. These two classes of choice situations may be called "single reinforcer" and "multiple reinforcer" respectively.

Model 3 offers two ways of treating the single-reinforcer choice situation. Suppose two bars are available, each with its own characteristic values for M, W, and N/n or N/t. An equilibrium value of n/t can be calculated for each bar separately. The choice problem is solved most easily by predicting that the subject will choose that bar for which n/t is minimal. Thus we would expect O to end up using only one of the bars and ignoring the other. This solution assumes that the subject will minimize his output in a choice situation. If n/t for each bar is equal, this solution predicts that O would spend equal amounts of time on each. In this way an indifference state could occur in such a choice situation.

This solution, however, assumes that O can discriminate the different values of n/t. A more sophisticated analysis of this choice problem could be obtained by making the choice behavior a probability function of the difference between the possible values of n/t.

In a multiple-reinforcer choice situation, Model 3 points to some singular complications. Suppose O has available two bars, one yielding food and another water. If we consider the schedule for the first bar, we see that O is reinforced at a certain rate for responding to that bar. But his responses to the bar yielding water are not reinforced by food, and these responses unreinforced by food must be added to the schedule prevailing on the food bar. If O is reinforced regularly on both bars, he actually is reinforced by food for *all* responses on a partial schedule. If his rates on both bars are equal, his food reinforcement schedule is effectively one reinforcement per two bar presses. Thus the multiple-reinforcer situation effectively shifts the schedules for all response possibilities, whatever schedule may be set externally for each one. Further development of Model 3 along these lines may enable a quantitative prediction of multiple-reinforcer choice behavior.

We shall briefly elaborate our discussion of the multiple-reinforcer situation to indicate some implications of this situation for extensions of the Hullian scheme.

Within the usual conceptual context of the Hullian analysis (in which we do not approach the problem in terms of behavioral equilibria and comparative statics), the introduction of several positive (rewarding) goals also complicates the analysis. When there is only one rewarding performance, the subject will presumably perform whenever $s\hat{E}r$ is above threshold. Suppose, however, that there are at least two responses, say R_1 and R_2, providing different goals such that at a particular moment both $\hat{E}_1$ and $\hat{E}_2$ are suprathreshold. Now, the probability that either R_1 or R_2 will be performed is equal to 1.[24] However, the probability that, say, R_1 will

24. This holds within the context of the usual Hullian-type analysis. As Dollard and Miller (1950, pp. 352–69) have pointed out, however, a subject confronted with two rewarding goals may for a time at least elect neither,

be performed is less than 1, the exact value depending upon the difference between $\bar{E}_1$ and $\bar{E}_2$. Let t_1, t_2, t_3, etc., denote the beginning of the first, second, third, etc., time periods. The outcome of performance in, say, t_2, will influence the performance in t_3, and the outcome of performance in t_3 will influence performance in t_4; and so on. Suppose the investigator has made observations upon the subject's learning history up to t_1, and now wishes to predict future performance upon the basis of just this much information. Presumably he could make a probabilistic prediction of the outcome to be expected during t_1. But what about t_2? Again presumably, he could make a probabilistic statement regarding the expected outcome in this period, but because a prediction about t_2 would hinge upon the probabilistic prediction concerning t_1, and a prediction concerning t_3 would depend upon probabilistic predictions concerning t_1 and t_2, and so on, there would be a rapid attenuation in the reliability of predictions. In other words, the existence of numerous goals would seem to decrease greatly the time horizon of prediction. More importantly, this consideration suggests the possibility that from a comparative-statics point of view the locus of new equilibrium positions may not be independent of the route from one to the other, and hence that predictions concerning the

---

rather remaining in some sort of behavioral equilibrium between the two. This will be the case if electing the one goal means giving up the other, and avoidance of the one (and of the other) is generated on this score. See their description of the double-approach-avoidance choice. This would seem to be a paradigm for the usual economic choice, i.e. in which the subject must allocate some scarce resource (money, time, energy, etc.) among a variety of competing ends. The difficulty with direct application of this analysis to many economic choices is this. The analysis serves to explain why it is that the subject *does not* elect one goal or another at a particular point in time. In many economic analyses, however, we wish to explain why the subject *does* elect one goal or the other at a certain time rate during a period of time. Presumably, in the double-approach-avoidance situation, the accumulation of drive with the passage of time would force some choice, and the next choice would be influenced by the drive reduction in consequence of the initial choice, etc. Again, as in our discussion of the free behavior situation, the explanation of continuing time rates of performance would seem to depend importantly upon some statements about the growth of drive and its decrease due to performance—more importantly, perhaps, upon this factor than upon those explicitly incorporated into the double-approach-avoidance analysis.

locus of new equilibrium positions cannot be made without knowledge about all the individual trials or episodes of behavior that presumably lead from one to the other. Of course, still within the usual Hullian type of analysis, the introduction of several rewarding performances results in a number of additional analytical difficulties, especially those of accounting for the effects of possible stimulus generalization.

Some general features of Model 3, including contrasts with Models 1 and 2, deserve comment before passing on to the multiple-organism situation.

First, there is the matter of the role of learning in Model 3. When a subject first enters a free behavior situation he responds at a low rate n/t. Reinforcement of his initial responses drives him out along the prevailing C_r or C_i function so that he responds at increasingly higher rates until the equilibrium point is reached. The D function keeps him from exceeding the equilibrium rate of n/t, and both the D function and law of effect keep him from falling below it. Similarly, when environmental variables change, O learns to adjust n/t to a new equilibrium value. "Learning" becomes no more than a name for the fact that O actually reaches equilibrium sooner or later.[25] Quantitatively, however, information regarding learning in controlled situations could be used to predict the *rate* at which O attains a new equilibrium. Learning occurs only when O meets new environmental constraints; and a theory of learning, when combined with Model 3, should enable prediction of the rate at which O's behavior will change when a new equilibrium is demanded by new constraints. We have not yet studied the mathematical aspects of this problem.

This treatment of learning contrasts somewhat with the treatment accorded this concept in Models 1 and 2. In all three models, behavioral equilibria are not attained until learning is complete. However, reverting to our earlier terminology, in which learning effects were identified with the positive effects of reinforced performance, Models 1 and

25. This is essentially the role ascribed to the learning process by Duesenberry (1949), who employs a learning-theory formulation to investigate the stability of a behavioral equilibrium established on other grounds.

2 attempted to carry over the positive effects of reinforced performance as determinative not only of the fact of reaching some behavioral equilibria but also of the locus of such positions. Thus Model 1 utilized the concept of K as one determinant of the locus of the final equilibrium position. Model 2 suggested two possibilities. One was that the positive effects of reinforced performance were determinative of the locus of equilibrium position, due to effects upon the n/t: B/t ratio. The other was that the positive effects were merely permissive, due to the fact that O"H" was assumed to have reached its limiting position. Since Model 3 utilizes only one motivation assumption, this model, even without further quantification, makes a prediction about the effects of an increase in magnitude of goal object upon n/t. This is not the case with Models 1 and 2, which utilize two opposing motivational assumptions.

These models also contrast with respect to the treatment accorded the influence of variations in work. Models 1 and 2 utilize only one assumption on this score, namely that increases in required work will tend to decrease tendency to perform because of the accumulations of work inhibition. Because of this single assumption, Models 1 and 2 can make a prediction about the effects of an increase in work upon n/t. Model 3, on the other hand, utilizes two assumptions about the effect of increases in work. One of these is that, at low rates of reinforcement, increases in work will tend to increase performance rates due to the effect of increasing the physiological requirements of the organism. The other is that, at high rates of reinforcement (the satiation asymptote), an increase in work will tend to decrease performance rates. This leads to the prediction that two D functions quantified under different work conditions will cross each other, the D function where work is greater lying to the right of the D function where work is less for n/t above the intersection point, and to the left of it for n/t below the intersection.

We have previously discussed the role played by the Hullian intervening variables in Models 1 and 2. In Model 3 Hull's intervening variables are used only to the extent of borrowing some notions involving motivation which appear in Hull's scheme and in systems offered by many other writers. Model 3 ignores work inhibition, incentive motivation, habit strength, and so forth. Insofar as these intervening variables are useful, they might enter Model 3 as parts of a learning theory to predict rate of attainment of a new equilibrium. The model could accommodate any other theory equally well, as long as that theory yielded predictions about n/t, and used N/t as one basis for such predictions. The test of Model 3 is, of course, the empirical program it suggests. We are quite certain that this program will force a substantial modification of the model. Its present form is only one of several possible first guesses regarding the quantitative relations between variables of simple free behavior situations.

CHAPTER 7

SOCIAL INTERACTION

IN the free behavior situations considered thus far only one organism has been involved. Most phenomena of interest to social scientists, however, are those arising from behavioral interaction between two or more organisms. The same problems found in the single-organism examples also may appear in such interaction situations. The variables which are considered antecedent or independent in classical S-R theory may themselves be functions of the behavior of the participants in interaction situations; these participants usually have a long learning history which would be difficult, if not impossible, actually to unravel; and we are generally interested in studying the time rate of performance of various responses. The additional complications found in studying interaction rest on the fact that the behavior of each participant is determined to some extent by the behavior of the others.

Often it is contended that the behavior of individuals or sets of individuals cannot be handled by S-R theories when the behavior to be predicted is a function of the behavior of others. This broad generalization may hold better for some kinds of interpersonal effects than for others.

When the influencing behavior has already occurred and can be described, its effects should in principle be subject to the same kind of analysis as are nonbehavioral conditions. Behavioral conditions are, however, much more complex than the kinds of stimuli typically studied by S-R theorists. Simply to describe them as stimuli or stimulus conditions does not tell us all we need to know about them. Thus far, S-R theorists who refer to "stimulus similarity" or "strength of stimulus" with reference to the stimulus properties of human behavior have usually used the terms for illustration or post hoc explanation, without specifying or using any operations by which such properties could be rigorously defined.

But if human behavior could be systematically related to stimulus values in an S-R theory, there is no reason why it could not be used for the kinds of prediction we have discussed. Indeed, it is difficult to imagine a theory of human behavior which failed to consider the behavior of others as an important determinant of the predicted behavior. It is significant that analyses which classify individuals on the basis of experience or exposure to conditions usually emphasize experience or conditions which result for the most part from the behavior of others.

More complicated than the effects of influencing behavior which has occurred in the past is the prediction of effects of behavior which will occur at some time after prediction. The simplest cases are those in which the investigator knows in advance how the influencers will act. This can be accomplished either through experimental instruction or by assumption in a situation where influencing behavior is known to follow predictable patterns. Even with such knowledge it is not easy to predict learning experiences. If the influencing behavior occurs without regard to the timing of the behavior of the predictee, it is difficult to predict what the temporal relation between the two will be. Since most S-R theories depend on timing (e.g. contiguity of stimulus and response, time of delay of reward), this makes prediction of relevant experiences difficult. If influencing behavior is fixed, in the sense that it occurs in some systematic relation to predictee's behavior, the free behavior situation remains a problem; i.e. predictee's experience is a function of his own behavior and vice versa.

Many empirical studies have been made of the behavior of individuals or sets in a specifiable interpersonal environment. Classic among these is the study of various "social climates" done under the direction of Kurt Lewin (1939) in which the effects on aggressive behavior of different kinds of leadership were studied. More recently, Asch (1951) has developed a design for studying behavior in the event of a conflict between the individual's sense perception and the reported perceptions of a group of which he is a member. In general, however, such studies have been more concerned with the group as a stimulus than with its effects in modifying response tendencies. More data on the latter process are needed before the utility of an S-R analysis in such problems can be evaluated.

Prediction of behavior of individuals and sets becomes particularly complicated when the influencing behavior of others must itself be predicted. In effect, this may be viewed as a situation in which the behavior of several individuals or members of several sets must be predicted as a function of the behavior of each other. If habit tendencies, and therefore behavior, change as a result of interaction during the period between prediction and performance, problems of prediction would be enormous. But even if change occurred only in the stimuli presented by each participant, prediction of the temporal sequence in which these would evoke and be evoked by responses of others would seem very difficult on the basis of an S-R theory. At present, therefore, it seems reasonable to attempt only the prediction of time rates of performance of various responses or classes of responses.

In the ensuing discussion of the problems involved in this type of analysis the following symbols will be used: A and B will denote individuals; Ra1 and Ra2 will represent different responses made by A, and Rb5 and Rb6 will represent responses made by B; S*Ra1 will represent stimuli created by Ra1 which are observable by B; S_1 and S_2 will represent stimuli whose occurrence for one individual is not contingent on the responses of other individuals.

A single interaction situation can be fully represented in principle by a sequence of the following sort involving A and B:

$$(S_1, S_2, S^*Ra1) — Rb5 — (S_2, S_3, S^*Rb5) — Ra2 — (S_3, S_4, S^*Ra2) — Rb8 — (S_3, S_2, S^*Rb8) — Ra15 — — —.$$

A complete analysis of this sequence would involve the use of a method enabling one to categorize responses and describe the stimulus situations preceding any response by an interactor A. This poses an exceedingly complicated problem which appears impossible to solve at present. A more complete analysis of interaction, however, shows that this problem can be considerably simplified.

In the first place, the analysis of one interaction situation is primarily aimed at the correlation between the S*Rai's and the Rbj's. Stimuli to B which do not depend on the behavior of A or vice versa can be temporarily set aside, since we are interested in how the behavior of A affects the behavior of B. Under the conditions just outlined, interaction analysis must work with the following sequence:

S*Ra1 — Rb5 — S*Rb5 — Ra2 — S*Ra2 —
Rb8 — S*Rb8 — Ra15 — — —.

This leaves us with the problem of categorizing responses and specifying stimuli which arise from the behavior of A or B. This latter requirement, however, is unnecessary if we make the following assumption: the physical stimuli S*Rai from any response Rai are always different from S*Raj arising from Raj when $i \neq j$, and are identical when $i = j$. This assumption in effect does away with the necessity of including the physical S*Ra1, S*Rb2, etc. in the description of an interaction sequence, and *it implies that one problem of analysis of interaction is to treat the correlations between the responses of A and those of B.* The time sequence of interest to interaction analysis is therefore:

Rb5 — Ra2 — Rb8 — Ra15 — — — — — — — — —.

The correlation between any Rai and its succeeding Rbj will not be perfect, however, for the following reasons: First, we have no guarantee that the probability of a response to a given stimulus is ever 1.00. The statistical properties of behavior may be such that a high correlation between stimulus and response is an infrequent occurrence among humans. Second, we have temporarily ignored the S_1, S_2, etc., the stimuli whose occurrence for B is not dependent on the behavior of A. Such stimuli will certainly affect behavior in the direction of lowering the intercorrelations between the Rai's and Rbj's. For our immediate purposes, however, we shall treat their effects as those of "random noise." In doing this we may by definition say that an interaction between two people, A and B, occurs when the correlations between the Rai's and Rbj's are at values above chance.

Throughout this discussion we have assumed that we have some system for categorizing responses made by each interactor. We have already discussed the problem of classifying responses (see Chap. 3). Given some such set of categories, we can ask first, what the correlations are between successive responses, and second, how the time rate of performance of each type of response changes during interaction. In studying these problems one may use pooled data for all interactors, or data for only one interactor at a time. We have discussed the first question above and will now turn to the second.

Many previous studies of interaction have concentrated on the prediction of whether, how quickly, and with how many errors (e.g. Shaw 1932; Preston, 1938) the interacting group will achieve some final goal, such as the solution of a problem. This is essentially a question of predicting the time distribution of certain classes of responses which may occur near the end of the interaction. The intercorrelations between responses, which were discussed previously, provide one way of making such a prediction.

Another method, not involving response-response correlations, is to study the time distribution of responses (Parsons, Bales, and Shils, 1953, pp. 111–40). S-R theory suggests certain variables which may influence the time distribution of a response or set of responses. These variables may be presumed to operate through the behavior of the interactors to influence the status of the interaction at any given time.

During an interaction sequence the rate of a response may be variously modified. The Hullian approach suggests that rate of performance is an increasing function of level of drive and amount of rewarded practice as well as of magnitude and immediacy of rewards. Interaction can affect each of these. An interactor (A) can heighten the level of an interactee's drive by presenting the latter (B) with painful or fearful stimuli or by depriving him of the opportunity to reduce his drive. Alternatively, A can contribute to the reduction of B's drive, in which case, according to a drive-reduction theory of reinforcement, he also tends to reinforce B's previous S-R sequences, increasing a given nonasymptotic rate to a degree related to the amount and immediacy of drive reduction. Thus prediction of changes in rate requires knowledge of the frequency with and extent to which A reinforces B, and of the timing of these reinforcements in relation to B's behavior.

Several factors may be expected to contribute to the determination of reinforcement through interaction. First among these is the level of B's drive, which may be low enough to preclude some kinds of reinforcement and minimize others. Drive level may have been reduced by previous interactions with A or other individuals, or by B's individual actions. Whatever drives B has may or may not be reducible by A, depending on the nature of the drives, on A's previous learning, and on environmental factors. If some action by A can afford reinforcement for B, then reinforcement of B's action is an increasing function of A's tendency to perform this, as opposed to competing, nonrewarding behavior. By his behavior, B can in turn affect the likelihood that A will reinforce him: by reinforcing and stimulating those of A's responses which are reinforcing to him and by not contributing to the evocation of incompatible responses.

Previous reinforcement of A's reinforcing response, whether or not given by B, would appear important in its effects not only on probability of occurrence but also in determining the immediacy and magnitude with which B is reinforced. Time of occurrence of a response is effected by its latency, which is correlated to some degree with rate. It is not unreasonable to suppose that reinforcement magnitude for B is affected by the vigor with which A performs the reinforcing response.

The effects of reinforcements given in an interaction situation have often been discussed under the rubrics of "copying" and "imitation." Miller and Dollard (1941), among others, have treated these mechanisms as special cases of general principles of learning. In their analysis they distinguish between matched-dependent and copying behavior. In the former the imitator's behavior is determined primarily by stimuli from the behavior of the organism imitated; in the latter the imitator's behavior becomes progressively more determined by cues from his own behavior which resemble cues from the model's behavior. By reinforcing the imitator for "correct" behavior the model insures that the stimuli from such behavior gain secondary reinforcing properties and that those stimuli are like the stimuli generated by the model's behavior. In this situation, stimuli from both the model's behavior and the imitator's behavior must be available to the latter. Generally, visual or auditory stimuli meet this condition. The correct sequence of responses develops by chaining each response to the stimuli generated by the preceding responses. In the case of matched-dependent behavior the organism acquires a new response sequence by chaining each response to the stimuli generated by the model's behavior; without the latter stimuli the imitator would be unable to perform correctly in a matched-dependent situation.

There is a third situation, however, which has not been analyzed in discussions of response development in humans: an instructor provides verbal stimuli to which a subject responds with a new sequence of behavior. In this situation the appropriate single responses have already been attached to the verbal cues offered by the instructor. The response chain would be developed by attaching each response to the cues of preceding responses.

A much more serious problem arises in studies of interaction and reinforcements given during interaction by the possible existence of a phenomenon which we shall label, for convenience, "vicarious learning." Workers in a number of disciplines have suggested that an increase in tendency to perform certain given behavior sometimes results from the mere observation of that behavior being performed by a second individual. Psychoanalytic literature is replete with references to the inclination of children to model their actions after adults (e.g. Erikson, 1950, pp. 210–13). An outstanding theory of role learning emphasizes the factor of "consistency with which others in the individual's environment exhibit to him the response called for by his role" (Cottrell, 1942b; see also 1942a). In economics it has been suggested, notably by

Duesenberry (1949, pp. 17–46), that observation of consumption by others increases the consumer's tendency to spend.

Among the many attempts to explain this phenomenon, a few have used concepts close to those of behavior theory. Duesenberry, for example, explains an increase in consumption following "demonstration" by another consumer in terms of an increased "drive to get higher quality goods." The stimulus of relative material inferiority presumably elicits a desire for consumption or a fear of status loss which can be reduced by consuming as much as the demonstrator. Miller and Dollard attribute copying to an acquired drive to copy which is reduced following behavior resembling that of the model. If this general approach is to be followed, it would be useful to know under what circumstances such drives occur as well as how they affect performance.

It seems likely that similarity or equivalence perceived by an individual between himself and the observed actor will prove to be one important determinant of the degree of learning to which such experiences give rise. Though the importance of this factor has long been noted (Giddings, 1896), little progress has been made toward its measurement or systematic inclusion in a theory of imitation. For the present we may be able to do little beyond obtaining its measures and using them as independent variables which determine implicit trials.

Ultimately it would be useful to be able to explain "perceived similarity" of actors in terms of the learning processes which affect it. One might postulate that implicit responses occur when behavior of others is observed, and that such responses are differentially rewarded, so that the observer learns to make them following the behavior of some, but not all, possible models. That differences in the types and numbers of models result from diverse social environments is strongly indicated in psychoanalytic materials on identification and in ethnological studies (Murdock, 1949b). It remains the task of a systematic theory of social behavior to show precisely how a given environment results in a particular pattern of vicarious learning.

So far we have treated the analysis of a single interaction situation largely in terms of the sequences of responses made by interactors. In doing this we have ignored the role of stimuli not contingent upon those responses. An actual analysis of interaction along the lines suggested here would have to take account of such stimuli. These stimuli are of two sorts. One type includes those which arise from the physical environment; the other includes stimuli presented by the interactors which are not contingent on behavior: appearance, age, physical size, and so forth. Many of these latter stimuli are correlated with general aspects of the behavior of the person affording them, and they may affect the behavior of others. Thus the group membership of an interactor is potentially an important factor which can aid prediction concerning rates of performance of responses and sequential correlations between responses.

Much empirical work in the social sciences has been based on the assumption that individuals who belong to groups tend to behave similarly. The ill-defined term "group" has been used to denote either an *organization*, i.e. an aggregate of mutually interactive individuals, or, more generally, a *set*, i.e. any aggregate of individuals differentiable from nonmembers by the possession of one or more common characteristics. Since all members of an organization have their membership as a common attribute, the first type of group is a special case of the second.

Organizations include families, various subsocietal units, and societies. Anthropologists have particularly emphasized the proposition that membership in a society makes for similarity in behavior. Exemplifying this point of view, Ralph Linton (1945, p. 20) states, "The fact that most members of [any particular] society will react to a given situation in a given way makes it possible to predict their behavior with a high degree of probability." The explanation of this similarity is to be found in terms of learning. Linton says further (1945, p. 14): "When several persons react in the same way to a particular situation, the cause must be sought in the experience which such individuals have in common. Obviously this fund of common experience will be much greater for the members of a single society than for members of different societies." Thus membership in a given society is seen as an attribute correlated with given learning experiences and therefore with similar behavior.

Among nonorganized sets as well, similarities in behavior have often been demonstrated. Social scientists have looked for empirical correlations of various forms of behavior with such attributes as sex, age, race, I.Q., occupation, education, residence, sibling position, and socialization. Correlations found by this method have often been left unexplained. It is possible that many of them may ultimately be explained in terms of the differential learning to which such attributes are related. An explanation of this sort would have to take account of several ways in which given characteristics affect learning. At the present stage we can only guess at these.

Membership in sets can affect behavior by giving rise to a similar learning history in several ways. Sets may be differentiated in the kinds of stimuli typically presented: finger bowls are far more frequently seen by upper- than by lower-class persons. Infrequent stimulus presentation limits the possible number of reinforced trials, so that learning may be less if a difficult skill must be acquired. Members of sets may also differ in the frequency with which they make a particular response to a given stimulus during learning. If learning can occur vicariously, however, overt performance may be supplemented by observation of overt behavior performed by others. Such observed behavior may also contribute to learning through copying, to which it is by definition indispensable. Members of sets may vary in the degree to which models are available for copying or vicarious learning. The result of differences in this regard is illustrated in the apparent difficulty found among boys brought up without a sociological father in learning to play the male role in our society.

Sets are also differentiable in regard to the frequency, magnitude, immediacy, and pattern with which reward follows a given stimulus-response sequence. Reinforcements are dependent on factors in both the material and social environments. Social environments are differentiated in the kinds of behavior they reward. Members of organizations typically learn to behave similarly. Some of their behavior usually has the effect of exerting positive and negative sanctions on the persons with whom they interact. To the extent that these controls are consistently exercised they will tend, other factors being equal, to reinforce certain S-R connections and make for the elimination of others. It is to be noted, however, that even within an interactive group differential controls are evoked by different sets of actors. Physical or behavioral characteristics may provide the basis for differential control reactions to the same behavior. In our society women (or Negroes or children, etc.) present stimuli which serve to evoke control reactions to given behavior different from those evoked by similarly behaving men (or whites or adults, etc.). Though often based upon a class of perceptible stimuli, differential controls may be evoked or supplemented by cue-producing responses, such as "This person is a criminal" or "That person is sick." The interrelations between these two types of stimuli and their connection with control responses deserve further study in such areas as class, race, and role relations.

Even where the same consequences follow given behavior for different sets, differential learning may result. One major reason for this lies in the fact that sets may differ in their members' values, i.e. the kinds of states of affairs which are rewarding or punishing to them.[1] While some value differences result from innate factors, such as those associated with age or sex, a majority would seem to depend on learning. As a result of earlier experience, one man's meat may come to be another man's poison. Work of some psychoanalysts in particular has recently been directed toward discerning the relationship of early experience to value systems (Kardiner et al., 1945), but further systematization in this area is called for. All too frequently, however, differential value systems, whether explained or merely described, have been taken as simple explanations of differences in behavior. As a correc-

1. For an alternative approach to the concept of value cf. Kluckhohn et al. (1951, pp. 388–433).

tive to this, further work is needed in exploring the interrelation of values and conditions of reinforcement in their effects on behavior.

Sets of individuals may also be differentiated in regard to their speed of learning under constant conditions of reinforcement. General differences in the so-called "learning constants" may be correlated with intelligence test scores and other measures of performance when these are applied following constant training.[2] It is possible that these constants also vary with the age of the actor, although this has not been conclusively established as independent of other learning (see Miles, 1933). As such tests are refined, it may be possible to show differences in the central tendencies of the learning constants of various sets. Such differences would be expected to contribute to differential behavior after a given number of trials, and, for certain behavior, even at the asymptote. It should be noted that differential speed of learning may also give rise to reactions on the part of others, toward slow as against fast learners, which sometimes lead through the control mechanisms mentioned above to major differences in the conditions of reinforcement typically confronted by members of different sets. An example is to be found in educational systems which adopt learning speed as a criterion for further training.

Differences in learning history resulting from these factors bear not only on the relevant reaction potentials themselves but also, by generalization, on potentials involving similar stimuli and responses. Though innate differences may exist between individuals in regard to the nature of their generalization gradients, these have not been adequately described. On the other hand, distinctive generalization gradients based upon learned equivalence or distinctiveness of stimuli[3] are characteristic of certain sets—for example, those comprising native speakers of a given language (Whorf, 1949) or individuals receiving similar verbal instructions (Birge, 1941).

2. Latency of a reaction following a given period of training has been shown to correlate negatively with intelligence (Peak and Boring, 1926; McFarland, 1937a, 1937b).

3. See the discussion of acquired equivalence in Miller and Dollard (1941, pp. 74–6).

Such differences may be expected to lead to differences in the strength of tendencies generalized from S-R connections of equal strength.

All these factors in the learning history of set members may affect their habit strengths and anticipated rewards in such a way as to provide them with distinctive reaction potentials. If their behavior is to be predicted at a given point in time, it would seem necessary to take into account, in addition to learning history, the present situation of members of a given set. This would include the nature of the stimuli currently being presented and the degree of drive present. Even if two sets are identical in regard to their reaction tendencies, presentation to them of nonequivalent stimuli usually evokes differential responses, while differences in degree of drive may lead two otherwise similar sets to tranquility or frenetic activity, as the case may be.

Each of these several factors would seem able individually to produce characteristic behavior in a given set. When combined, their effects become very difficult to predict. Thus, members of a given society who have high drive but little previous reinforcement for fighting may have the same momentary effective reaction potential to go to war as a neighboring society under the same conditions with low drive but much previous reinforcement for warlike behavior. Without a quantitative system, it would seem impossible to predict which would be more likely to fight.

In the real world, sets which are of greatest interest typically are differentiated by a number of these characteristics. Psychologists might be aware of these when in their experiments they assume that "cultural factors" are constant. For their part, nonlaboratory social scientists are to be commended when they seek to isolate the factors contributing to differential behavior of such sets as races, classes, and members of various occupational and familial statuses. Whether this effort can be aided by a learning approach remains to be demonstrated.

In the analysis outlined here we have tried to point out the actual operations that seem to be involved in studying interaction. A theoretical description of interaction would include the stimuli S*Raj in order to permit statements about stimulus generalization. But stimulus similarity in interaction could also be treated as a direct function of the physical similarity of the responses giving rise to those stimuli if an adequate method of categorizing responses were available. This, again, might help to simplify the operational problems of observing interaction, although it would not change the theoretical analysis which might be made. Acquired similarity of stimuli, however, would probably render an approach this simple inadequate, and in dealing with responses where acquired similarity of response-produced stimuli is involved it would be necessary operationally to reintroduce S*Raj into the operations used in observing behavior.

The problem of stimulus similarity is also complicated by another factor: the type of response categorization used. Different categorizations will split actual behavior in different ways and thus generate different descriptions of interaction and similarities between interaction sequences.

Finally we must point out that we have chosen to approach interaction from a theory of individual behavior in the hope that its consequences will be deducible from that theory. For this reason some of our terminology will seem different from that employed by theorists who have taken as their starting point the analysis of interaction per se. That the results are not incompatible, however, is suggested by the fact that variables in some of these systems may be interpreted in our terms.[4]

4. A number of systems permit this kind of treatment, but we shall confine ourselves to only one illustration.

In his systematic sociology, Talcott Parsons (1951; Parsons and Shils et al., 1951, pp. 47–279; Parsons, Bales, and Shils, 1953) has classified interactions according to five pattern variables: affectivity, collectivity, universalism, achievement, and specificity. For our purposes we may concentrate on the experiences to which these refer. The following translations show the rough correspondence between terms of the two systems: affectivity—immediacy of reward; collectivity—importance of rewarding interactees; universalism—generalization of behavior to a class of interactees; achievement—dependence of A's behavior on stimuli provided by B's *responses* (rather than other nonresponsive attributes); specificity—limitation of interactive responses through the selection of stimuli. Each of these five variables is placed by Parsons in three systems, cultural, personality, and social; that is, the actor may be normatively obliged, desire, and be expected on probable

The advantage of such translation goes beyond the facilitation of communication between social scientists. It holds out the hope that nonoperational variables which are taken as independent in other theories may become definable and dependent in relation to operationally definable psychological variables.[5] With the aid of an explicit set of postulates relating these variables it should become possible to predict the experiences affecting previously independent variables.

---

pain of sanction to perform a given kind of interaction. "Normative obligation" seems to refer to verbal descriptions obtainable from members of the social group as to correct or desirable behavior. "Desire" is roughly analogous to reaction potential. Expectation might be given behavioral definition in terms of the likelihood of reward for performance or punishment for nonperformance of given behavior.

5. For a criticism of the Parsons-Shils theory in terms of its failure to explain the pattern variables see Swanson (1953).

CHAPTER 8

CULTURAL BEHAVIOR AND STIMULUS-RESPONSE THEORIES

THIS book has been largely concerned with long-run developmental problems in social behavior science. We feel that the problems raised are important ones from this point of view, and also that profitable discussion of them is not barred by the fact that many of these problems will probably not be resolved in the near future. Nevertheless, many social scientists are understandably interested in the matter of what results a given theory can deliver to them tomorrow or the next day, in addition to the matter of what results the same theory may deliver at some unspecified future time when certain of its current problems have been satisfactorily resolved. In consequence we feel it desirable to make a few statements relative to the former matter. For the most part these statements will be general ones. However, brief descriptions of two attempts to analyze particular behavioral processes in stimulus-response terms have been included.

At the outset of this section it must be observed that in inquiring into the applicability of psychological theory to human cultural behavior (i.e. behavior which is learned by one human being from another), we are dealing with an issue which has been the subject of strong and conflicting opinions among social scientists. Many have maintained that psychological postulates are inadequate or misleading when applied to most sociological and anthropological data. Durkheim (1950) attacked sociological dependence on the individual psychology of his era in the following terms: ". . . because society is composed only of individuals, the common-sense view still holds that sociology is a superstructure built upon the substratum of the individual consciousness . . . [but]

the mentality of groups is not the same as that of individuals; it has its own laws." Subsequent writers have also criticized those who accept "the notion that to explain sociological phenomena they must reduce them to psychological phenomena" (Lundberg, 1939; Apple, 1951). Perhaps the most extreme anthropological view of the matter is set forth by White (1949, pp. 140–1) who declares that "Culture must be explained in terms of culture . . . not in terms of psychology. . . . The most realistic and scientifically adequate interpretation of culture is one that proceeds *as if* human beings did not exist."

On the other hand, human cultural behavior has often been described in terms which suggest its susceptibility to individual psychological analyses. Sumner (1906, p. iv) was among the first to do this with his definition of folkways as "habits of the individual and customs of the society which arise from efforts to satisfy needs." The same emphasis is found in C. S. Ford's description of culture as "traditional ways of solving problems . . . responses which have been accepted because they have met with success; in brief, culture consists of learned problem solutions" (Ford, 1942, pp. 547, 555, 557). The latter definition, characterized by Kroeber and Kluckhohn as expressing the central tendency of psychologically oriented views of culture,[1] has been criticized by them on the grounds that "everything characteristically cultural has been dissolved out of Ford's definitions except . . . 'traditional.' The drift is to resolve or reduce culture into psychology" (Kroeber and Kluckhohn, 1952).

A compromise view is proposed by Kroeber, who holds that "at present it is equally impossible to explain culture in terms of individual psychology and to understand it without some reference to psychology. After all, culture exists only through persons, in or by their behavior. Yet when we study culture, we concern ourselves primarily with those aspects of behavior which are more than individual. Our generalizations, and therefore our specific scientific findings, are obviously on a more-than-individual level. But the individual and per-

1. For a systematic discussion of possible definitions of culture see Moore (1952).

sonalized substratum is still there" (Kroeber, 1948, p. 577; see also Parsons, 1951, pp. 552–3).

We think that the real issues in this controversy have all too often been obscured by mutual misunderstandings by the participants. Very few scientists would be willing to accept either of the following statements: No psychological theory can contribute anything to the understanding of any cultural behavior, or All cultural behavior may be fully accounted for by an extant psychological theory. Most would take the position, which we here assume, that some but probably not all cultural behavior may be usefully analyzed in terms of some theory of individual psychology.

The question for us then becomes, What kinds of cultural behavior can be fruitfully analyzed in these terms? Though no conclusive answer can now be made, it should be possible to clarify the question. In order to do this it will be necessary to distinguish and discuss the kinds of theory referred to, and to discuss whether the behavior to be predicted is that of an individual or of some aggregate.

First we would like to limit our discussion to a particular kind of psychology. Discussants on both sides of this issue often fail to specify the kind of psychological theory which they feel is or is not applicable to cultural behavior. Though of obvious importance, it is often crucially unclear whether by "psychology" is meant theories having to do with instincts, faculties, personality traits, fields, associations, fixations, or theories involving some combination of these. Instead of using the general term "psychology," we shall therefore limit ourselves to a discussion of a particular class of psychological theories, namely those which seek to predict the behavior of a given individual in a particular situation on the basis of his prior experiences in behaving in a given way under similar conditions. These may be roughly designated as "stimulus-response" or "S-R" theories.

Second, we should specify what kinds of phenomena are to be dealt with. Despite occasional disclaimers it is clear that most social-science activity is directed toward the study of some form of, consequence of, or inference from someone's behavior. The behavior in question may be that of a specific individual, that of members of a category or set of not necessarily interacting persons having one or more characteristics in common, or that of an interactive aggregate or "group" of persons. Diverse problems arise from attempts to theorize about these different combinations of persons whose behavior is to be studied.

In what has gone before we have pointed out that stimulus-response psychology has concentrated, in principle at least, upon behavioral changes consequent upon the behavioral experience of individual organisms in the context of an impersonal environment. The qualification "in principle" is necessitated by circumstances which require observations upon the performance of groups of organisms if these observations are to constitute a test of the theory suggesting them, even if the focus of interest is to draw inferences about individual behavior per se. Of course, predictions in social science may be useful for reasons in addition to the one that such predictions may constitute a test of the theory suggesting them; for example, as a basis for policy decisions (in which an attempt may be made to control the phenomenon under consideration). Thus explanations of individual performance based upon suitable life learning histories of a particular organism may be useful. Several excellent life histories are at hand which suggest that such prediction may be fruitful (e.g. Radin, 1926; Dyk, 1938, 1947; Shaw, 1930; Dollard, 1935).

However useful individual studies may be for certain purposes, it is clear that for reasons of both interest and necessity much social science activity is aimed at obtaining correlations between the (in some sense average) behavior of aggregates of individuals and specified stimulus conditions, or between some attributes of such aggregates and some other attributes of such aggregates. Generally speaking, this is likewise a considerable portion of the scientific activity in the area of S-R psychology. Whether other areas of study may expect assistance in this activity from S-R psychology turns in part upon the nature of the problem in question.[2] To this matter we now turn.

2. We will neglect many, sometimes important, contributions which S-R psychology can make to investigators in other fields. For example, an exposure to S-R psychology, which, in part because of the possibility of

The criteria in terms of which individuals may be, and have been, aggregated into sets are numerous and depend on the kinds of problem the aggregator faces. Analysis consists in correlating some attributes of such a set with some other attributes of such a set, or some average behavior of such a set with some stimulus conditions, or some antecedent conditions pertaining to such a set with some behavior of such a set, and so forth. Whether stimulus-response theory can assist or supplement such analyses depends mainly upon two things: 1. whether elements in the analysis can be identified with elements in the S-R formulation, and 2. whether, once this identification is made, the empirical content of the S-R theoretical formulation is relevant to the problem at hand. Obviously, then, the hope of assistance from S-R theory depends greatly upon the particular problem at hand, and no over-all generalization can be made on this count.

A favorable instance is afforded by recent work (in terms of environment-inferred experience-based sets) of Whiting and Child (1953). They were interested in predicting typical explanations of illness in a number of societies, using concepts from Hull and Freud. People holding such typical beliefs in a given society were assumed to have been subjected as children to current socialization customs, defined as characteristic habits of a typical socializer in the society. A set was then formed on the basis of the severity or indulgence with which a given kind of socialization (e.g. weaning, toilet training, control of aggression) was presumed to have been administered. A set whose members were severely trained in regard to an item such as heterosexual play, for example, would include those individuals who presumably were punished when and if they were found engaged in this kind of

---

experimental control, emphasizes operational definitions of response events and empirical testing of hypotheses, is apt to make an investigator much more careful about these matters with respect to the data and techniques which he is accustomed to using. As a positive contribution along these lines, the terminology employed in S-R psychology often provides a vehicle in terms of which concepts can be expressed in an unambiguous way, understandable to investigators in diverse fields. We neglect such matters because they perhaps have more to do with the sociology of scientific investigators than with technical integration as such.

activity. This kind of set is thus based on a presumption of some specific experience. Using such sets as a basis for classification, Whiting and Child found significant correlations between childhood experience and theories of illness.

This was a favorable case because elements in the analyses (including aggregation criteria upon which set membership was based) were readily identifiable with theoretical elements in the systems of Hull and Freud. Further, the empirical content of these systems (that is, the phenomenal referents of the theoretical elements) was seemingly sufficient for the analysis in question.

It must be expected, however, that many more cases will be unfavorable. This is sometimes because elements in the usual analysis cannot readily be identified with theoretical elements in S-R psychology. (A good bit of our prior discussion has had a direct bearing upon this point. See, for example, our discussion of the difficulty of identifying reinforcers, Chap. 4, pp. 68 ff.)

Often, however, the reason for this is that S-R psychology, in its present stage of development, simply does not have the right kind of empirical data input to its theoretical formulations to permit their utilization, even if identification with the theoretical elements of the formulation seems possible. An example of this kind of situation may be found in economics, which is, by reason of the phenomena in which it is interested, about as favorable a general social science context for the possible application of S-R psychology as can be found. For one thing, behavior can often be measured in terms of quantities (e.g. goods bought or sold, hours worked, revenue expended, proportion of expenditure to income, which suggest a scaling of strength of tendency to perform. Furthermore, elements in an analysis of acquisition and/or disposition of material goods and services, and the like, can often be identified with antecedent conditions relating to drive, reward consequent upon performance, etc. Nevertheless the economist attempting to apply S-R psychology to particular economic problems will usually find that (in addition to obstacles discussed earlier in this book) detailed application is precluded by the lack of empirical content relevant to the problem at hand. For example, the analysis may strongly imply that the behavior in question is importantly dependent upon the drive status of the subject. But of what antecedent conditions may the drive status of the subject be said to be a function? From the point of view of empirical content, the Hullian formulation suggests a few possibilities, e.g. food and water deprivation, but rudimentary deprivation and "strong stimulus" conceptions of drive are seldom helpful in the analysis of the social economic behavior of subjects with long learning histories who are greatly influenced by secondary motivations.

Problems of theoretical formulation and of data input have been faced by workers who have attempted to apply Hullian analysis to complex social data. In general, the solution has been to utilize Hullian variables without specifying any rigorously defined set of operations by which these variables can be measured. For example, though the concept of drive is usually used, its presence and degree are identified in various ways.

Gillin (1945) seeks to connect an acquired drive to primary drive. "Among the Indians [in a Guatemalan community] the money-drive is based closely upon innate drives of hunger and pain. An Indian wants money to buy food, shelter, and clothing, and to avoid the actual physical punishment which is involved in failure to pay taxes, rents, and other obligations." In another set, the Ladinos, the money drive is acquired partly through the capacity of money to bring prestige.

Whiting (1941) is concerned chiefly with the primary drive of pain, whose presence is inferred from the application of physical force. In this he follows the first part of Miller and Dollard's (1941, p. 18) definition of drive as "a strong stimulus which impels action." In dealing with acquired drives, however, Whiting depends at least in part on the second part of the definition. Thus he infers the drive properties of the Kwoma phrase *karaganda yikafa* from two facts: that it is frequently used in conjunction with physical punishment and deprivation and that it can be used to motivate toleration of pain. The latter criterion appears to be used as an indication of amount of drive: "The fact that Kwoma children will mutilate their penises and willingly undergo scarification in order not to be classified as *karaganda yikafa* indicates the motivational power of this concept" (Whiting, 1941, p. 185).

Another method is used by Dollard in his discussion of diffusion (Miller and Dollard, 1941, pp. 253–73), when he apparently infers the existence of acquired drives from the presence of behavior which persistently results in the attainment of a given object. "Hunger is characteristic of all societies, but a secondary drive or appetite for acorns characterized the Indians of California, for the meat of the bison the Indians of the Great Plains, for salmon the dwellers of the northwest coast of America, etc." (Miller and Dollard, 1941, p. 256.) Though the implication is clear that hunger is the primary drive on the basis of which these drives are acquired, their presence is inferred from behavior rather than from evidence of systematic conditioning.

Schwartz (1954) discusses selection and training of his populations as factors which would be expected to make public disapproval a greater "loss" to members of an Israeli collective than it would be to members of a comparable semiprivate village. This "expectation is confirmed," according to the writer, by verbal responses to a Guttman scale indicating that adult members of the collective are more likely to follow public opinion in the event that it conflicts with their own inclinations. The relation between these test scores and training history as criteria for loss is, however, left indeterminate, a resolution which is possible only where, as there, they converge. In the event of divergence between these two criteria, one should be explicitly accepted as defining the variable.

All these studies have been post hoc attempts to explain phenomena already known by their writers to exist. Ultimately, prediction is the way of testing a theory. Attempts to formulate theories dealing with specific kinds of social behavior, namely lexical innovation and social control, have been made by members of our group. A brief discussion of these will serve to point out some of the problems and possibilities facing those who would utilize Hullian theory for such purposes.

An example of an attempt to formulate an integrated theory of human social phenomena is the theory of lexical innovation.[3] A lexeme occurrent in the idiolect of some members of a speech community but not others is a "test word." A speaker who uses a test word is a "model." A speaker who does not use the test word is a "tory." When a tory adopts a test word from a model, lexical innovation is said to have taken place. Note that lexical innovation is not descriptive of the coinage of items but only of their spread from speaker to speaker.

The factors postulated as important in lexical innovation are:

1. The phonemic regularity of the test word (R_p).
2. The morphemic regularity of the test word (R_m).
3. The status differential of model (x) over tory (y) ($S_{x/y}$).
4. The upward mobility of the tory (y) (M_y).
5. The frequency of interaction between model and tory (F_I).
6. The frequency of occurrence of the test word in the idiolect of the model in interaction with the tory (F_a).

The likelihood (L) that a tory (y) will adopt the test word from a model (x) is stated, in terms of the above factors, tentatively as follows:

$$L = (gR_p)\ (eF_I)\ (fF_a)\ (bR_m + cS_{x/y} + dM_y),$$

where b, c, d, e, f, and g are empirical constants providing slack against misweighting the variables by arbitrary measuring devices.[4]

The techniques proposed for obtaining values for the variables are drawn partly from linguistics and partly from current sociological and anthropological practice.[5]

3. For a more detailed statement of the theory see Olmsted (1954b).

4. We do not discuss here why some relationships of variables are presented as multiplicative, others as additive. These are, at best, only hunches at present, and are more fully discussed in the work cited above.

5. A research project designed to test the theory is at present under way among the Achumawi of northeastern California.

Among the actual predictive theorems resulting from these postulates are the following:

1. Other factors being equal, a tory will adopt the phonemically more regular of two test words more rapidly than he will adopt the phonemically less regular one.

2. Other factors being equal, a tory will adopt a test word supplied by a model x more rapidly than he will adopt one from a model w if the status of x is higher than that of w.

3. Other factors being equal, tory y will adopt a test word more rapidly than will tory z if the upward mobility of y is greater than that of z.

4. Other factors being equal, a tory will adopt the more frequently presented of two test words more rapidly than he will adopt the less frequently presented one.

The relation of these postulates to Hullian theory is at present twofold. First, their author has been influenced by Hull's use of deductive theory. This is a type of integrative benefit which has been noted above. It should be pointed out, however, that this general method, though neatly exemplified by Hull, is sufficiently widespread so as not to constitute a distinctly Hullian contribution.

Second, some variables and some relations between variables have been suggested by Hullian theory and by Miller and Dollard's (1941, 1950) discussion of it. Thus the postulates on phonemic and morphemic regularity are suggested by the stimulus generalization concept; those having to do with status differential and upward mobility may presumably be related respectively to incentive and drive; and the final factors may be said to reflect opportunities for rewarded trials.

It is significant, however, that the postulates of this theory have not themselves been formally deduced as theorems from Hull's theory. The author has taken, as operations for defining and obtaining values for the variables, research techniques available in such disciplines as linguistics, sociology, and anthropology. It is by no means clear that these operations will yield data which bear consistent and simple relations to the Hullian variables. To assume such relations seemed quite unnecessary for purposes of this theory.

An attempt to deduce a theory about social behavior from Hullian postulates reveals some of the difficulties entailed in such a process. One of the present writers has attempted to develop a theory of legal sanction in this manner.[6]

Sanction is defined as interactive behavior which serves to modify the drive level of the interactee. Sanction is positive when it reduces drive, and negative when it increases it. Legal sanctions are those imposed by specialists acting in their socially recognized and supported capacity as controllers of intragroup disturbance. Disturbance is any drive increment consequent upon a given behavior; intensity of disturbance refers to the degree to which drive is increased, while extensity refers to the proportion of persons in the social group who experience some disturbance.

The rate of disturbing behavior is a decreasing function of the immediacy, frequency, and magnitude of (potential disturbers') drive reduction following behavior incompatible with the disturbing behavior. A decline in this rate can be brought about directly by the administration of positive sanctions after such incompatible behavior. The likelihood of such a decline can also be increased by the administration of negative sanctions following disturbing behavior, since the higher the drive created the greater will be the possible magnitude of drive reduction upon a switch to incompatible behavior. These sanctions tend to modify not only the behavior of those who experience them directly but also of those who may be deterred through vicarious learning (see Chap. 6). Together with collateral (nonsanction) rewards and punishments they often have to offset the effect of sanctions for socially disturbing behavior which are provided by subgroups, as well as the effects of the reduction of physiological and other drives for which socially acceptable channels have not been found.

If single performances of given behavior effect a constant extensity and (mean) intensity of disturbance, then any decrease in the rate of performance will result in a decline in disturbance. Such a decline might be expected to reinforce those sanctions which preceded it as an increasing

6. For a summary of the theory see Schwartz (1954).

function of the immediacy, frequency, and magnitude with which disturbance declines. Disturbance decline is, of course, only one of the consequences which can reinforce the performance of a given sanction. The likelihood that a given sanction will be employed against a given kind of behavior is an increasing function of the degree to which such reinforcements have occurred upon its previous employment [7] and of the degree of similarity perceived by sanctioners between the behavior previously subjected to control and the given behavior. Competing reactions (e.g. withdrawal without sanction) will, to the extent that they have been reinforced, further diminish the likelihood of a given sanction being performed.

This theory suggests several problems in the application of Hullian theory to social behavior:

1. The Hullian definition of drive, in terms of hours of deprivation, seems unsatisfactory for the measure of most acquired drives. The drive concept, moreover, frequently bars prediction of changes in the rate of disturbing acts by predicting simultaneous decline in drive and reinforcement for nondisturbing acts. Until and unless these relations can be quantified, it would seem more fruitful to consider drive primarily in its bearing on reinforcement.

2. Human verbal processes force a reconsideration of Hullian definitions of time of delay of reinforcement and similarity of stimuli. Particularly important in this regard is the place of verbal norms. These appear to give cues to sanctionees which decrease anticipated reward for a given act. At the same time such cues serve to discriminate between sanctionable and nonsanctionable behavior, which under some conditions increases the possibility of a similar reaction by sanctioners.

3. States of affairs which reinforce human responses are so variable (from person to person and for a given person through time) as to require new research techniques. Choice

7. It is also deducible that such reactions will be relatively vigorous and have low latency. All of these measures will tend to contribute to a reduction of the disturbing behavior. It follows that reactions reinforced most strongly in the past will be employed in such a way as to be more likely to be reinforced.

between states of affairs is proposed as the basis for an operational definition of reinforcement, in preference to the "history of the organism" method.

4. Further problems arise from the attempt to predict social action as a function of disturbance reduction. Prediction is now attempted of the action of some individuals who are supported by others. Some index must be obtained of the capacity of a given individual to support others, since some individuals in a group have a greater power potential than others.

It would seem therefore that major innovations are required for an analysis of complex social behavior. One distinctively Hullian assumption is used, namely that the response measures are intercorrelated. This has permitted the deduction given in note 7. Though our discussion of this postulate suggests that it may not be universally correct (see Chap. 3), it would appear useful for the analysis of much social behavior. With this exception, however, only a few general notions, such as reinforcement and stimulus generalization, are retained. Neither of these concepts is uniquely Hullian, each being found in the earlier S-R theories of Thorndike and Pavlov. What has been used in this, as in the other works inspired by Hull, involves primarily these general notions. It is these which we consider the most useful parts of Hullian theory.

CHAPTER 9

SUMMARY

IN the foregoing chapters we have tried to formulate and discuss those issues which seemed to us crucial for application of stimulus-response psychology to cultural behavior. The observable variables of this psychological approach are stimulus and antecedent conditions, including the immediate environment of an organism, the organism's motivation, history of reinforcements, and responses. We have discussed techniques for operationally defining these variables in a general enough way so that they can be used in studying human social phenomena. We emphasized the advantages and problems arising from the observer's use of his own natural language in making these definitions.

After discussing antecedent conditions and responses, we made a preliminary attempt to deal with language and free behavior situations from an S-R point of view. We approached problem-solving situations in terms of the interplay between language and other variables in those situations. This approach produced a tentative analysis of the relations between the structure and use of language and environmental variables in problem situations. Under the term "free behavior situations," we suggested several models for analyzing behavior in cases where traditional independent variables, like motivation, are not experimentally controlled. These models suggest that the distinction between independent and dependent variables, which psychology so often uses, may be expendable without loss of the ability to predict behavior quantitatively. Furthermore, these models suggest a fairly extensive research program.

Finally, we also discussed problems involved in extending the particular S-R theory developed by Hull and his followers to cultural behavior. No single conclusion is dictated by our work as to the likelihood that Hullian theory will prove to be the most satisfactory basis for a general theory of human social behavior. Major divergences are to be found among the present authors on this score. One view holds that the Hullian theory as it now stands or as it may conceivably be modified probably cannot make any unique contribution to what is now known in social science and to what will be formulated in other theories. Another position holds that Hullian theory provides the best starting point for a general behavior science. We all agree that it provides at least a means of summarizing many of the empirical generalizations known to S-R psychology, and that these generalizations themselves provide a promising first step toward the integration of the social sciences.

GLOSSARY OF SYMBOLS

B	A theoretical unit of "seeking or striving behavior" in Free Behavior Model 2.
C_i	Fixed interval schedule of reinforcement.
C_r	Fixed ratio schedule of reinforcement.
D	Drive, based on h; or rate of reinforcement.
"D"	Motivation factor in Free Behavior Model 2.
E	Same as sEr, E_1, E_2 . . . for specific responses.
$\bar{E}$	Same as s$\bar{E}$r, $\bar{E}_1$, $\bar{E}_2$ . . . for specific responses.
$\hat{E}$	Same as s$\hat{E}$r, $\hat{E}_1$, $\hat{E}_2$ . . . for specific responses.
F_a	Frequency of test word in idiolect of model.
F_I	Frequency of interaction between model and tory.
"H"	Associative factor in Free Behavior Model 2.
h	Hours of deprivation.
H	Same as sHr.
I	Same as I_r.
Ir	Reactive inhibition, based on amount of work.
K	Incentive motivation in Hull's system, based on reinforcement.
L	Likelihood of adoption of a test word.
M	Magnitude of reinforcement.
M_y	Mobility of y.
N	Total number of reinforced responses.
n	Total number of responses, reinforced or not.
N/t	Rate of reinforced responses.
n/t	Rate of responding.
O	A subject.
P	Preference, as in R_1PR_2: R_1 preferred to R_2.
p	Probability.
Q	Speed.
R	Response; R_1, R_2 . . . specific responses.
Ral, Rb2	Specific responses made by individuals A and B in an interaction sequence.

R_G — Observable goal responses (eating, drinking, etc.).

R_m — Morphemic regularity of a test word (not a response).

R_p — Phonemic regularity of test word (not a response).

r — Theoretical response variable in Hull's system, isomorphic with R.

r_G — Theoretical goal response.

r_g — Fractional part of r_G.

r_p — Theoretical perceptual response.

S — Stimulus, S_1, S_2 . . . specific stimuli.

S-R — Stimulus-response, as in stimulus-response theory or stimulus-response sequence.

S_D — Drive stimuli.

S*Ral, S*Rb2 — Stimuli provided one individual by the response of another in interaction.

$S_{x/y}$ — Status differential of model over tory.

s — Stimulus trace, in Hull's system.

sEr — Excitatory potential, product of D, sHr, and K.

$s\bar{E}r$ — Effective excitatory potential, $sEr - (Ir + sIr)$.

$s\dot{\bar{E}}r$ — Response tendency, $s\bar{E}r - sOr$.

sHr — Habit strength, based on number of reinforced trials.

sIr — Conditioned inhibition, based on number of nonreinforced trials.

sKr — Suggested modification of K.

sOr — Behavioral oscillation.

T_G — Delay of reinforcement.

t — Time.

W — Work, in Free Behavior Model 3.

Wg — Weight of the goal object.

x, w — Model in lexical innovation.

y, z — Tory in lexical innovation.

BIBLIOGRAPHY

Adams, W. A. See No. 142.

1. Alchian, A. A. (1950) Uncertainty, evolution, and economic theory. *J. Polit. Econ.*, *58*, 211–21.
2. Alchian, A. A. (1953) The meaning of utility measurement. *Amer. Econ. Rev.*, *43*, 26–50.

Anderson, S. B. See No. 92.

3. Apple, D. (1951) Learning theory and socialization. *Amer. Sociol. Rev.*, *16*, 23–7.
4. Arrow, K. J. (1951) Mathematical models in the social sciences. In Lerner, D., and Lasswell, H. D., eds., *The policy sciences*. Stanford, Stanford Univ. Press. Pp. 129–54.
5. Bakke, E. W., and Argyris, C. (1954) *Organizational structure and dynamics*. New Haven, Labor and Management Center, Yale Univ.
6. Bales, R. F. (1951) *Interaction process analysis*. Cambridge, Mass., Addison Wesley Press.
   See also No. 104.
7. Bergmann, G., and Spence, K. W. (1941) Operationism and theory in psychology. *Psychol. Rev.*, *48*, 1–14.
8. Birdwhistell, R. L. (1952) *Introduction to kinesics: an annotation system for analysis of body motion and gesture*. Washington, D.C., Foreign Service Institute, Dept. of State.
9. Birge, J. S. (1941) Verbal responses in transfer. (Ph.D. dissertation, Yale Univ.)
10. Bloch, B. (1948) A set of postulates for phonemic analysis. *Language*, *24*, 3–46.
11. Bloch, B. (1950) Studies in colloquial Japanese IV: phonemics. *Language*, *26*, 86–125.
12. Bloch, B. (1953) Theme and variations. Presidential address, Linguistic Society of America. (Unpublished.)

Boring, E. G. See No. 106.

13. Boulding, K. E. (1950) *A reconstruction of economics*. New York, Wiley.

14. Buxton, C. E. (1940) Latent learning and the goal gradient hypothesis. *Contributions to Psychol. Theory, 2*, No. 2.

Carmichael, L. See No. 83.

15. Carnap, R. (1950) *Logical foundations of probability.* Chicago, Univ. of Chicago Press.

16. Carroll, J. B. (1953) The transitional probabilities of English phonemes: a preliminary report. Cambridge, Mass. (Mimeographed.)

17. Carroll, J. B., et al. (1951) Report and recommendations of the interdisciplinary summer seminar in psychology and linguistics. Ithaca, New York. (Mimeographed.)

Cartwright, D. See No. 71.

Cason, H. See No. 135.

Child, I. L. See No. 148.

18. Cottrell, L. S., Jr. (1942) The adjustment of the individual to his age and sex roles. *Amer. Sociol. Rev., 7*, 617–20.

19. Dollard, J. (1935) *Criteria for the life history.* New Haven, Yale Univ. Press.
See also No. 90.

20. Dollard, J., and Miller, N. E. (1950) *Personality and psychotherapy.* New York, McGraw-Hill.

21. Doob, L. W. (1947) The behavior of attitudes. *Psychol. Rev. 54*, 135–56.

22. Duesenberry, J. S. (1949) *Income, saving, and the theory of consumer behavior.* Cambridge, Harvard Univ. Press.

23. Durkheim, E. (1950) *The rules of sociological method.* Solovay and Mueller, trans. Glencoe, Ill., Free Press.

24. Dyk, W. (1938) *Son of old man hat.* New York, Harcourt, Brace.

25. Dyk, W. (1947) *A Navaho autobiography.* New York, Viking Fund Publications in Anthropology, No. 8.

26. Ehrenfreund, D. (1952) A study of the transposition gradient. *J. Exp. Psychol., 43*, 81–7.

27. Erikson, E. H. (1950) *Childhood and society.* New York, Norton.

28. Estes, W. (1950) Toward a statistical theory of learning. *Psychol. Rev.*, *57*, 94–120.

Fant, C. G. See No. 56.

29. Ford, C. S. (1942) Culture and human behavior. *Sci. Mon.*, *55*, 546–57.

30. Freud, S. (1938) *Basic writings of Sigmund Freud.* New York, Modern Library.

31. Gellhorn, E. (1953) *Physiological foundations of neurology and psychiatry.* Minneapolis, Univ. of Minn. Press.

32. Giddings, F. H. (1896) *Principles of sociology.* New York, Macmillan.

33. Gillin, J. (1945) Parallel cultures and the inhibitions to acculturation in a Guatemalan community. *Social Forces*, *24*, 1–14.

34. Gladstone, A. I., et al. (1947) Some functional relationships of reaction potential ($_{S}E_{R}$) and related phenomena. *J. Exp. Psychol.*, *37*, 510–26.

35. Grinker, R. (1946) *Neurology.* 3d ed. Springfield, Ill., C. C. Thomas.

36. Hall, E. T., and Trager, G. L. (1953) *The analysis of culture.* Washington, D.C., American Council of Learned Societies.

Halle, M. See No. 56.

37. Harlow, H. F. (1950) Analysis of discrimination learning by monkeys. *J. Exp. Psychol.*, *40*, 26–39.

38. Harris, Z. S. (1951) *Methods in structural linguistics.* Chicago, Univ. of Chicago Press.

39. Hebb, D. O. (1949) *The organization of behavior.* New York, Wiley.

40. Herskovits, M. J. (1948) *Man and his works.* New York, Knopf.

41. Hjelmslev, L. (1943) Prolegomena to a theory of language. Whitfield, F. J., trans. *International J. Amer. Linguistics*, Memoir 7. Baltimore, Waverly Press, 1953.

42. Hockett, C. F. (1942) A system of descriptive phonology. *Language*, *18*, 3–21.

43. Hockett, C. F. (1950) Age grading and linguistic continuity. *Language*, *26*, 449–57.

44. Hovland, C. I. (1937) The generalization of conditioned responses. I. The sensory generalization of conditioned responses with varying frequencies of tone. *J. Gen. Psychol.*, *17*, 125–48.
45. Howes, D. H., and Osgood, C. E. (1954) On the combination of associative probabilities in linguistic contexts. *Amer. J. Psychol.*, *67*, 241–58.
46. Hull, C. L. (1930) Knowledge and purpose as habit mechanisms. *Psychol. Rev.*, *37*, 511–25.
47. Hull, C. L. (1939) The problem of stimulus equivalence in behavior theory. *Psychol. Rev.*, *46*, 9–30.
48. Hull, C. L. (1943a) *Principles of behavior.* New York, Appleton-Century.
49. Hull, C. L. (1943b) The problem of intervening variables in molar behavior theory. *Psychol. Rev.*, *50*, 273–91.
50. Hull, C. L. (1951) *Essentials of behavior.* New Haven, Yale Univ. Press.
51. Hull, C. L. (1952) *A behavior system.* New Haven, Yale Univ. Press.
52. Hull, C. L., et al. (1940) *Mathematico-deductive theory of rote learning.* New Haven, Yale Univ. Press.
53. Hull, C. L., et al. (1947) A proposed quantification of habit strength. *Psychol. Rev.*, *54*, 237–54.
54. Hurlock, E. B. (1927) The use of group rivalry as an incentive. *J. Abnorm. and Soc. Psychol.*, *22*, 278–90.
55. Jakobson, R. (1941) *Kindersprache, aphasie und allgemeine lautgesetze.* Uppsala, Almquist & Wiksells.
56. Jakobson, R., Fant, C. G., and Halle, M. (1952) *Preliminaries to speech analysis: the distinctive features and their correlates.* Technical Report No. 13, Cambridge, Mass., Acoustics Lab., M.I.T.
57. Joos, M. (1948) *Acoustic phonetics.* Lang. Monogr., No. 23. Baltimore, Waverly Press.

Junker, B. H. See No. 142.

Kaplon, M. D. See No. 152.

58. Kardiner, A., et al. (1945) *Psychological frontiers of society.* New York, Columbia Univ. Press.

59. Kluckhohn, C. (1949) *Mirror for man.* New York, Whittlesey House.
See also No. 64.

60. Kluckhohn, C., et al. (1952) Values and value orientations in the theory of action. In Parsons, T., and Shils, E. A., eds., *Toward a general theory of action.* Cambridge, Harvard Univ. Press. Pp. 388–433.

61. Klüver, H. (1933) *Behavior mechanisms in monkeys.* Chicago, Univ. of Chicago Press.

62. Köhler, W. (1947) *Gestalt psychology.* New York, Liveright.

63. Kroeber, A. L. (1948) *Anthropology.* New York, Harcourt, Brace.

64. Kroeber, A. L., and Kluckhohn, C. (1952) *Culture, a critical review of concepts and definitions.* Papers of the Peabody Museum, Harvard Univ., *47*, No. 1, Cambridge.

65. Kurtz, K. H. (1953) Transfer of discrimination training with complex stimuli. (Ph.D. dissertation, Yale Univ.)

66. LaPiere, R. T. (1934) Attitudes vs. actions. *Social Forces, 13*, 230–7.

67. LaPiere, R. T. (1938) Sociological significance of measurable attitudes. *Amer. Sociol. Rev., 3*, 175–82.

68. Lashley, K. S. (1938) The mechanism of vision: xv. Preliminary studies of the rat's capacity for detailed vision. *J. Gen. Psychol., 18*, 123–93.

69. Leopold, W. F. (1937–49) *Speech development of a bilingual child.* Evanston, Northwestern Univ. Press, Vols. *1–4*.

70. Leopold, W. F. (1952) *Bibliography of child language.* Evanston, Northwestern Univ. Press.

71. Lewin, K. (1951) *Field theory in social science.* Cartwright, D., ed. New York, Harper.

72. Lindahl, L. G. (1945) Movement analysis as an industrial training method. *J. Appl. Psychol., 29*, 420–36.

73. Linton, R. (1945) *The cultural background of personality.* New York, Appleton-Century.

74. Lloyd, D. P. C. (1949) Post-tetanic potentiation of re-

sponse in monosynaptic reflex pathways of the spinal cord. *J. Gen. Physiol.*, *32*, 147–70.

75. Logan, F. A. (1951) A comparison of avoidance and non-avoidance eyelid conditioning. *J. Exp. Psychol.*, *42*, 390–3.
76. Logan, F. A. (1952) The role of delay of reinforcement in determining reaction potential. *J. Exp. Psychol.*, *43*, 393–9.
77. Logan, F. A. (1953) Psychological laws and theory for social scientists. (Unpublished.)
78. Luchins, A. S. (1942) Mechanization in problem solving. *Psychol. Monogr.*, *54*, No. 248.
79. Lundberg, G. A. (1939) *Foundations of sociology.* New York, Macmillan.
80. Maier, N. R. F. (1940) The behavior mechanisms concerned with problem solving. *Psychol. Rev.*, *47*, 43–58.
81. Marx, M. H. (1951) The general nature of theory construction. In Marx, M. H., ed. *Psychological theory.* New York, Macmillan. Pp. 4–19.
82. May, M. A. (1917) The mechanism of controlled association. *Arch. Psychol.*, *5*, No. 39.
83. McCarthy, D. (1946) Language development in children. In Carmichael, L., ed. *Manual of child psychology.* New York, Wiley.
84. McFarland, R. A. (1937a) Psychophysiological studies at high altitudes in the Andes. I and II. *J. Comp. Psychol.*, *23*, 191–258.
85. McFarland, R. A. (1937b) Psychophysiological studies at high altitudes in the Andes. III and IV. *J. Comp. Psychol.*, *24*, 147–220.
86. McGeoch, J. A. (1942) *The psychology of human learning.* New York, Longmans, Green.
87. McNemar, Q. (1946) Opinion-attitude methodology. *Psychol. Bull.*, *43*, 289–374.
88. Miles, W. R. (1933) Age and human ability. *Psychol. Rev.*, *40*, 99–123.
89. Miller, G. A. (1951) *Language and communication.* New York, McGraw-Hill.

Miller, N. E. See No. 20.

90. Miller, N. E., and Dollard, J. (1941) *Social learning and imitation.* New Haven, Yale Univ. Press.

91. Moore, O. K. (1952) Nominal definitions of culture. *Phil. Sci., 19,* 245–56.
See also No. 101.

92. Moore, O. K., and Anderson, S. B. (1954) Search behavior in individual and group problem solving. *Amer. Sociol. Rev., 19,* 702–14.

93. Moore, O. K., and Olmsted, D. L. (1952) Language and Professor Levi-Strauss. *Amer. Anthrop., 54,* 116–19.

94. Mosteller, F., et al. (1949) *The pre-election polls of 1948.* New York, Social Science Research Council.

95. Mowrer, O. H., et al. (1951) Symposium on learning. *Psychol. Rev., 58,* 350–86.

96. Muenzinger, K. F., and Powloski, R. F. (1951) Motivation in learning: x. Comparison of electric shock for correct turns in a corrective and a noncorrective situation. *J. Exp. Psychol., 42,* 118–24.

97. Murdock, G. P. (1949a) Science of human learning, society, culture, and personality. *Sci. Mo., 69,* 377–81.

98. Murdock, G. P. (1949b) *Social structure.* New York, Macmillan.

99. Olmsted, D. L. (1953) Review of A. L. Kroeber, ed. Anthropology today. *Language, 29,* 590–7.

100. Olmsted, D. L. (1954) *Toward a cultural theory of lexical innovation: a research design.* Georgetown University Monograph Series on Languages and Linguistics, 7, 105–17.
See also No. 93.

101. Olmsted, D. L., and Moore, O. K. (1952) Language, psychology, and linguistics. *Psychol. Rev., 59,* 414–20.

Osgood, C. E. See No. 45.

102. Osgood, C. E., ed. (1954) *Psycholinguistics: a survey of theory research problems.* Baltimore, Waverly Press.

103. Parsons, T. (1951) *The social system.* Glencoe, Ill., Free Press.

104. Parsons, T., Bales, R. F., and Shils, E. A. (1953) *Working papers in the theory of action.* Glencoe, Ill., Free Press.

105. Parsons, T., and Shils, E. A., eds. (1952) *Toward a general theory of action.* Cambridge, Harvard Univ. Press. See also No. 60.

106. Peak, H., and Boring, E. G. (1926) The factor of speed in intelligence. *J. Exp. Psychol.*, *9*, 71–94.

107. Perin, C. T. (1942) Behavior potentiality as a joint function of the amount of training and the degree of hunger at the time of extinction. *J. Exp. Psychol.*, *30*, 93–113.

Powloski, R. F. See No. 96.

108. Radin, P. (1926) *Crashing thunder, the autobiography of an American Indian.* New York, Appleton.

109. Ramond, C. K. (1954) Performance in selective learning as a function of hunger. *J. Exp. Psychol.*, *48*, 265–70.

110. Riesen, A. H. (1947) The development of visual perception in man and chimpanzee. *Science*, *106*, 107–8.

111. Robbins, L. (1930) On the elasticity of demand for income in terms of effort. *Economics*, *10*, 123–9.

Roby, T. B. See No. 118.

112. Samuelson, P. A. (1947) *Foundations of economic analysis.* Cambridge, Harvard Univ. Press.

113. Schmidt, H. O. (1941) The effects of praise and blame as incentives to learning. *Psychol. Monogr.*, *53*, No. 240.

114. Schwartz, R. D. (1954) Social factors in the development of legal control: a case study of two Israeli settlements. *Yale Law J.*, *63*, 471–91.

115. Sells, S. B. (1936) The atmosphere effect: an experimental study of reasoning. *Arch. Psychol.*, *28*, No. 200.

116. Shaw, C. R. (1930) *The Jack roller: a delinquent boy's own story.* Chicago, Univ. of Chicago Press.

117. Sheffield, F. D. (1948) Avoidance training and the contiguity principle. *J. Comp. Physiol. Psychol.*, *41*, 165–77.

118. Sheffield, F. D., and Roby, T. B. (1950) Reward value of a nonnutritive sweet taste. *J. Comp. Physiol. Psychol.*, *43*, 471–81.

119. Sherrington, Sir C. S. (1947) *The integrative action of the nervous system.* 2d ed. New Haven, Yale Univ. Press.

Shils, E. A. See Nos. 104, 105.

120. Skinner, B. F. (1938) *The behavior of organisms.* New York, Appleton-Century.
121. Skinner, B. F. (1950) Are theories of learning necessary? *Psychol. Rev., 57,* 193–216.
122. Skinner, B. F. (1953) *Science and human behavior.* New York, Macmillan.
Smith, H. L., Jr. See No. 134.
123. Spence, K. W. (1936) The nature of discrimination learning in animals. *Psychol. Rev., 43,* 427–49.
124. Spence, K. W. (1937) The differential response in animals to stimuli varying within a single dimension. *Psychol. Rev., 44,* 430–44.
125. Spence, K. W. (1940) Continuous versus noncontinuous interpretations of discrimination learning. *Psychol. Rev., 47,* 271–88.
126. Spence, K. W. (1944) The nature of theory construction in contemporary psychology. *Psychol. Rev., 51,* 47–68.
127. Spence, K. W. (1951) Theoretical interpretations of learning. In C. P. Stone, ed. *Comparative psychology.* 3d ed. New York, Prentice-Hall.
See also No. 7.
128. Stevens, S. S. (1939) Psychology and the science of science. *Psychol. Bull., 36,* 221–63.
129. Stevens, S. S., ed. (1951) *Handbook of experimental psychology.* New York, Wiley.
Stone, C. P. See No. 127.
130. Stouffer, S. A., et al. (1950) *Measurement and prediction.* Princeton, Princeton Univ. Press.
131. Sumner, W. G. (1906) *Folkways.* Boston, Ginn.
132. Swanson, G. E. (1953) The approach to a general theory of action by Parsons and Shils. *Amer. Sociol. Rev., 18,* 125–34.
133. Thurstone, L. L. (1927) A law of comparative judgment. *Psychol. Rev., 34,* 273–86.
Trager, G. L. See No. 36.
134. Trager, G. L., and Smith, H. L., Jr. (1951) *An outline of English structure.* Studies in linguistics. Occasional Papers, No. 3, Norman, Okla., Battenburg Press.

135. Trowbridge, M. H., and Cason, H. (1932) An experimental study of Thorndike's theory of learning. *J. Gen. Psychol.*, *7*, 245–60.

136. Trubetzkoy, N. S. (1939) *Grundzüge der phonologie.* Prague, Czechoslovakia, Cercle Linguistique de Prague.

137. Twaddell, W. F. (1935) *On defining the phoneme.* Lang. Monogr., No. 16, Baltimore, Waverly Press.

138. Underwood, B. J. (1949) *Experimental psychology.* New York, Appleton-Century-Crofts.
See also No. 151.

139. Voegelin, C. F. (1951) Culture, language, and the human organism. *Southwestern J. Anthrop.*, *7*, 370.

140. Wallin, P. (1949) An appraisal of some methodological aspects of the Kinsey report. *Amer. Sociol. Rev.*, *14*, 197–210.

141. Ward, L. B. (1937) Reminiscence and rote learning. *Psychol. Monogr.*, *49*, No. 220.

142. Warner, W. L., Junker, B. H., and Adams, W. A. (1941) *Color and human nature.* Washington, D. C., American Council on Education.

143. Weber, E. H. (1846) Der tastsinn und das gemeingefühl. In Wagner, R. (1842–53), *Handwörterbuch der Physiologie.* Braunschweig, Germany, F. Vieweg und Sohn, *3*, Pt. 2, 481–588.

144. Wertheimer, M. (1945) *Productive thinking.* New York, Harper.

145. White, L. A. (1940) The symbol: the origin and basis of human behavior. *Philos. Science*, *7*, 451–63. Reprinted in White, L. A. (1949) *The science of culture.* New York, Farrar, Straus, pp. 22–39.

146. White, L. A. (1949) *The science of culture.* New York, Farrar, Straus.

Whitfield, F. J. See No. 41.

147. Whiting, J. W. M. (1941) *Becoming a Kwoma: teaching and learning in a New Guinea tribe.* New Haven, Yale Univ. Press.

148. Whiting, J. W. M., and Child, I. L. (1953) *Child training and personality: a cross-cultural study.* New Haven, Yale Univ. Press.

149. Whorf, B. L. (1949) *Four articles on metalinguistics.* Washington, D. C., Foreign Service Institute, Dept. of State.

150. Williams, S. B. (1938) Resistance to extinction as a function of the number of reinforcements. *J. Exp. Psychol.*, *23*, 506–21.

151. Wilson, J. T. (1948) The formation and retention of remote associations in rote learning. (Unpublished Ph.D. dissertation, Stanford Univ.) As summarized in Underwood, B. J. (1949) *Experimental psychology.* New York, Appleton-Century. P. 422.

152. Wolfe, J. B., and Kaplon, M. D. (1941) Effect of amount of reward and consummative activity on learning in chickens. *J. Comp. Psychol.*, *31*, 353–61.

153. Woodworth, R. S. (1938) *Experimental psychology.* New York, Henry Holt.

154. Zeaman, D. (1949) Response latency as a function of the amount of reinforcement. *J. Exp. Psychol.*, *39*, 466–83.

INDEX

BOOKS, IN PRINT, PUBLISHED BY THE YALE UNIVERSITY PRESS FOR THE INSTITUTE OF HUMAN RELATIONS